Also by Albion Press:

How To Investigate Your Friends And Enemies

MAKE THE JERK PAY

Tracking Down A Deadbeat Dad And Getting Child Support

Louis J. Rose and Roy Malone

Published by: Albion Press
9701 Twincrest Drive
St. Louis, MO 63126.
1-888-787-4477 (toll free)

Printed in the United States of America.

This publication is designed to provide useful information and is sold with the understanding that the authors are not engaged in rendering legal or other professional services. State laws vary and a competent professional should be consulted when a reader requires expert assistance or legal advice.

The authors and Albion Press specifically disclaim any liability or responsibility to any person regarding any loss or damage caused or alleged to be caused directly or indirectly by the information contained herein.

Publisher's Cataloging-in-Publication
(Provided by Quality Books, Inc.)

Rose, Louis J., 1931 –
Make the jerk pay: tracking down a deadbeat dad and getting child support/ by Louis J. Rose and Roy Malone.
—1st ed.
p. cm.
Includes index.
Preassigned LCCN: 98-93329
ISBN: 0-9606846-3-8

1. Child support – Law and legislation – United States – Popular works.
2. Missing persons – Investigations – United States. I. Malone, Roy. II. Title.

KF549.Z9R67 1999 346.7301'72
QBI98-1026

DEDICATION

We dedicate this book to the millions of children who deserve child support but are not getting it. Many are living in poverty. We hope this book will help single parents obtain the financial support their children need.

ACKNOWLEDGMENTS

A number of friends and colleagues have made this book possible. We thank **Tony Lazorko,** news art director at the St. Louis Post-Dispatch, who handled page production, interior and cover design. His wife, **Marge Biddle,** assisted.

Special thanks are due **Fred W. Lindecke,** who edited the book and helped prepare it for production. Computer expert **Virgil Tipton** wrote most of the chapter dealing with the Internet. Others who helped are attorney **Mark Sableman** and newspaper colleagues **Larry Fiquette, Jan Paul, Kathleen Flynn, Mike Crowley** and **Lewis Schucart.** Also, we thank members of the ACES organization, including **Geraldine Jensen** and **Debbie Kline.**

Louis Rose thanks his family members for their support: his wife, **Carol Rose,** their daughter **Leslie Rose Howell,** and their son, **John J. Rose.** Roy Malone's wife, **Carol,** also deserves thanks.

Unpaid child support is "a national disgrace, an unbelievable problem causing child poverty."

— ***Geraldine Jensen,***
president of ACES, The Association For Children For Enforcement of Support

"Failure to pay child support is the largest single crime in the United States."

— ***Carole A. Chambers,***
author of Child Support: How To Get What Your Child Needs and Deserves

One father sent in a death certificate to prove he had died. A man in Illinois transferred a business into his mother's name. Another father copied his brother's birth certificate and took on his identity. A dentist moved seven times in one year, finally ending up in South America.

—***St. Louis Post-Dispatch***

"Texas child support is a joke. But my kids aren't laughing. Their father is."

— *Sign carried by picketing mother whose ex-husband owed $8,000 in back child support.*

"We call them bums, because that's what (deadbeat dads) are,"

—***John Blosser***
of the National Enquirer, who has written about parents who deliberately avoid paying child support.

PREFACE

This book takes a hard look at the reasons the government bureaucracy has failed as the nation's bill collector for child support.... and how families get their money in only about one in five cases.

It's a national scandal that millions of fathers don't pay and get away with it. Their ex-wives and children often end up on welfare.

This book is valuable to single parents who need help in getting the child support they are entitled to. It offers help on how to obtain support, so that your family won't end up victims of a deadbeat dad, or in some cases, a deadbeat mom.

Make The Jerk Pay goes beyond just explaining how to use the child support enforcement system. It tells how you can track down a missing spouse by using your own skills and available public records. Beyond that, you will learn how to do some sleuthing to uncover money, property and other assets of the deadbeat.

Men may take offense at the book's title. But we consider it justified because nine out of ten deadbeats are men. For the custodial fathers trying to collect from deadbeat moms, this book is for you, too.

> Many deadbeat fathers refuse to pay because of their anger toward their ex-spouses. It's their way of getting even. But mothers must avoid the trap of letting hostility undermine their efforts to find the absent fathers and get them to pay.
>
> Keep in mind that your goal isn't revenge, but to do what is best for your children. This takes not only determination, but a cool, methodical approach.

Some men won't admit they're the fathers. Others simply don't care. Too many husbands don't want the responsibility of being a father, so they end up divorcing their children as well as their wives. They run off, often moving from state to state. Some create new identities for themselves by changing their names and getting new Social Security numbers, new credit cards and driver's licenses.

They go to great lengths to conceal their assets from the families they abandon, sometimes putting property in the names of others. Many arrange to be paid under the table so their earnings cannot be traced or attached. Often they will flout court orders to pay child support — knowing they're likely to get away with it.

The tactics of deadbeat dads add up to a nightmare, financially and emotionally, for the mothers and children. Too often the mothers are left to fend for themselves at a time when they are least able to cope.

Many women will not even seek child support. They may fear hostility from their husbands, or feel that asking for child support is like asking for a handout. Others shy away because they fear it will be costly, time-consuming and too much of a hassle to deal with the bureaucratic child support system.

If you are such a victim, you may feel abandoned and cheated. That's natural. Some women strike back by denying visitation rights to the father. That's a mistake. It hurts the child and gives the absent father an excuse for not paying child support.

But you need not feel powerless. There are laws and state and county agencies that are supposed to help you. It's the responsibility of prosecutors and judges to aid you in getting support orders and enforcing them. You can turn to support groups whose members know exactly what you are going through and can help you cope with the system.

In the end, it's up to you to help find him and make him pay. Because you have the most at stake, you may have to become a squeaky wheel and pester child support officials to get your case moving.

There are countless mothers who have made the system work for them. You will read vignettes about some of those women and how they triumphed, often by the force of their will.

Lou Rose
Roy Malone
St. Louis

CONTENTS

PART 1

AMERICA'S SHAME: CHILDREN ABANDONED

PART 1

AMERICA'S SHAME: CHILDREN ABANDONED

1

NON-SUPPORT IS A NATIONAL DISGRACE

America's child support system is in chaos. One in every four children lives in poverty, largely because an absent parent — usually the father — can't or won't pay child support.

Millions of children are being shortchanged by a growing army of deadbeat dads who hide themselves and their assets from their children. Upward of $40 billion in unpaid child support has piled up. About 11 million families are owed support. Taxpayers are picking up a huge tab each year for the nearly 10 million children forced onto welfare rolls. The biggest single cause is that 16 million children are living in homes without fathers.

Many of these are getting no support from their dads. And — by the government's own figures — the problem isn't going away.

CHILDREN GET SUPPORT IN ONLY ONE OF FIVE CASES

A federal panel depicted the states' system of collecting child support as a "cumbersome, slow-moving dinosaur fed by paper." Most states are doing a poor job of collecting. Overall, they collect in only 19 percent of the cases.

But finally, after decades of getting inadequate attention, the problems linked to non-payment of child support are being recognized as a social issue that demands action by government at all levels. It will also require a change in attitude on the part of parents who shirk their responsibility.

Like drunk driving or drug abuse, the damage done to families by absent parents who don't support their children is increasingly spotlighted in the media. One woman in a California-based child advocacy group, summed it up:

"Once there was no stigma attached to drunk driving. Now there is. That's what we'd like to do with child support. We want to make it unacceptable to not pay your child support."

Many single mothers get discouraged when they try to use the child-support collection system but hit a wall of indifference. The odds are heavily against them. Time and again they are frustrated by over-burdened caseworkers and prosecutors who ignore their cases and by irresponsible fathers who know they can get away without paying.

Sometimes women can't get the system to locate the fathers. A former NAACP official told a federal panel about problems in one southern state:

"Alabama is hooked up to several computer-location services but local child support caseworkers tell their clients that they themselves must locate the absent parent before any action can be taken on their case. We have a District Attorney.... (who) actually tells clients in writing that they must draw a map to the absent parent's home before any action can be taken on their behalf."

SOME MOTHERS WHO BEAT THE ODDS

Following are mothers who hit the wall, but didn't quit. In later chapters we'll detail their stories.

BELINDA MCGRATH couldn't find her ex-husband and wrote off any chance of collecting court-ordered support for her two daughters. She was living in a mobile home near Detroit and went on welfare for a year. "I lived out of suitcases and boxes," she said. She got training at a business college and went to work for a small firm while her mother watched the kids.

McGrath

At first she didn't want to have anything to do with her ex-husband. But later she changed her mind. "I was quite angry," she said. "I decided I would go after him for child support." She still didn't know where he was. Then one day she read a newspaper article about finding deadbeat dads. She was on her way.

NANCY SISSONS of Glen Cove, Long Island, tried for nine years to make her ex-husband, an engineer, pay support. The total owed climbed to $40,000. He moved from state to state, but she couldn't pin him

Sissons

down long enough to collect. She was told her chances were hopeless. Throughout, she had to work two jobs to provide for her two daughters.

Then a girlfriend in Texas mentioned a firm that might be able to help her track down the errant father and collect from him. "I was a little bit leery of it, to tell the truth, but I didn't have anything to lose," Sissons said. She decided to try it, and is glad she did.

Jensen

GERALDINE JENSEN was infuriated when she left the child support enforcement office in Toledo. A surly worker there had berated her for demanding more help to collect about $12,000 in back payments that her ex-husband owed their two young sons. For years Jensen had worked two jobs, but lost her home.

"I'm so tired of you women coming in here, whining and complaining," the man told her. "If you think you can do a better job, go do it." It was the final insult after being shuffled about by bureaucrats. She had only $12. She used most of it for a classified newspaper ad which said: "Not receiving your child support? Call me." Thus began her fight to help thousands of beleaguered mothers by starting ACES, the national self-help group for collecting child support.

Bennett

PAT BENNETT had two small daughters, no money or job, and was pregnant again when her husband walked out. Despite a court order, he paid less than $100 and disappeared. He changed his name, assuming another man's identity. She knew she would track him down some day. But it would take a while to get emotionally ready.

In the meantime, she had to go on welfare for two years. She got financial help from her parents and took college courses in business and accounting. She then began a 15-year search, tracking her ex-husband from Virginia to Texas and finally to Florida where he was arrested. Her compelling story was told in a book, a movie and before a congressional committee.

Woolsey

LYNN WOOLSEY said she once lived a "Leave It To Beaver" life in an affluent California community. After she was divorced, her ex-husband, a stockbroker, never paid a penny in support. She had to go on welfare to help raise her three children. It was before there was a child support system.

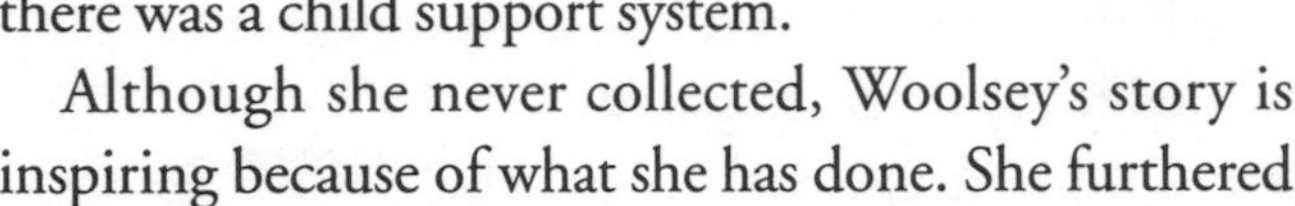

Although she never collected, Woolsey's story is inspiring because of what she has done. She furthered her education, ran her own business and got into politics. As a congresswoman from north of San Francisco she speaks from experience while pressing Congress to reform the child support system. She says collections would be greatly increased if the IRS handled them.

2

JERKS RUN — KIDS SUFFER

The family unit has been eroded in the last few decades as never before in this country. The main reasons are dramatic increases in divorce and children born out of wedlock.

Many parents respond with a growing sense of bitterness and hopelessness as they see their families breaking down. In many cases, fathers seem to react with total indifference as they abandon their children.

Nearly half of all marriages end in divorce. Over three decades — from 1950 through 1981 — the divorce rate more than doubled.

In recent years, the number of divorces has leveled off slightly, but has routinely topped the 1-million mark. In 1995, for example, the nation recorded 1.17 million divorces, according to the Statistical Abstract of the United States.

More than one in four mothers today have never been married — up from one in twenty in 1960. More than 10 million women — including three million divorced mothers — are raising children without the father in the home.

Divorce and separation hits the mother harder than the father. On average, mothers who are left with bringing up children see their income drop, while absent fathers have more to spend on themselves, rather than on their children.

THE COSTS OF ABANDONMENT

Besides welfare, the costs to society can be measured in other ways. Children in poverty are often more susceptible to social problems such as drug and alcohol abuse, teen pregnancy, gang pressures, homelessness, criminal behavior, and failure to get an education. Again, it's the taxpayer who ends up paying.

Children are hurt emotionally when they are abandoned by a parent. One girl told a congressional commission of the pain she and her brothers experienced:

"My mom has been working at a full-time job that barely pays over minimum wage. She is going back to school at night to get a better job.... we hardly get to see her, so instead of losing just one parent, we lost two."

Children may feel guilty about the breakup of the parents and their mothers' economic plight. They often suffer from being caught in the middle of bitter fights over custody and visitation. Dr. Lee Combrinck-Graham, a child psychiatrist, told Parents magazine that parental infighting can devastate children.

"When a child is aware of tension between his parents over child-support payments, he is bound to take upon himself a large amount of the responsibility for trying to make things better between them," the doctor said. Combrinck-Graham said parents should understand that they must not use children as a weapon in their fights.

THE DEADBEAT DAD MENTALITY

Too often, men father children without providing for their care. It has become so commonplace that it carries no stigma. The trend may span two or three generations within a family, sociologists say.

A soda bottler in St. Louis stymied officials when they pursued him for child support. The man had fathered 22 children out of wedlock and had three more with his wife. "He's employed, but we can't take any more of his money," said a perplexed John Dockery, an assistant prosecutor in charge of the city's child-support enforcement unit.

Many absent dads spend more in a year on car payments than on their children. Their ranks include doctors and lawyers who can easily afford to help their children. They do not recognize any moral or legal obligation to provide for their children.

Some are immature and walk away from their families out of sheer selfishness, perhaps born of the "me now" generation.

Take the case of Jeffrey Nichols, an investment adviser earning about $400,000 a year who was dubbed the nation's No. 1 Deadbeat Dad by the media. He evaded paying back support of more than $600,000 by moving from New York to Florida, to Canada, and finally to Vermont.

Nichols lived a lavish lifestyle with a new wife while failing to pay support for his three children whom he hadn't seen in several years. At one point he said he was sterile and claimed he wasn't their father; tests confirmed he was.

After he was arrested by the FBI, Nichols told a judge all he owned was a gold watch, office machines, and some clothing, and he was heavily in debt. The judge didn't buy it. Property from his expensive home was later sold at auction to satisfy some of the back support. His former wife, Marilyn Nichols Kane, said, "This was a man who valued things over people."

ON THE RUN

Some fathers resort to creating a new identity. They may get a driver's license under another name and a different Social Security number or birth certificate. Some have pretended they died, including one who turned in a death certificate to prove it.

But an impostor can still be caught. **Take Gary Elliott.** He deserted his wife and family in Coffeen, Illinois, and made it look like he had died — the victim of foul play. He took the name of a boy who died 26 years earlier. Police in California discovered his true identity 14 years later in a routine investigation. In all that time he never gave his seven children a cent. Nice guy.

Another deadbeat who changed his name to avoid paying $60,000 to his three kids in Connecticut got caught when he called his ex-wife. She got his number off her telephone's Caller ID function. Police traced the number to a residence in Missouri. He was arrested and charged with felony non-support.

Other deadbeats settle down in their new states, remarry and spend their time and money on their new families. They avoid paying anything to their earlier families and hide assets in the names of relatives or friends. They change jobs frequently and often work for cash.

Nina J. Easton, writing in the Los Angeles Times, cited the case of a father who said he couldn't pay his child support. His reason: "He needed the money to board his two pure-bred Doberman pinschers." Another father, Easton wrote, "was furious because prosecutors seized his Rolls Royce to partly cover $200,000 in back child and spousal support."

One man, she said, claimed he was no longer the father because he had had a sex-change operation.

In Missouri, a man was charged with deliberately injecting his one-year-old son with HIV-tainted blood. Prosecutors alleged the man's motive was to avoid paying $267 a month in child support. By age five, the boy had full-blown AIDS.

The greater the conflict between separated parents the less likely it is that child support will be paid.

WHY WOULD A FATHER TURN HIS BACK ON HIS CHILD?

There's no single reason. Many men don't know what it means to be a good father because their own fathers — if they even knew them — treated them shabbily and were poor role models. Some men never really develop any relationship with their children, so they don't feel guilty about not supporting them.

For some fathers, not paying child support becomes a weapon in a continuing fight with the ex-wife. For her part, the mother may refuse or restrict visitation rights. As the battle escalates, the father becomes more and more alienated from his family, and stops sending payments.

Frank Furstenberg, a sociologist and author of *Divided Families*, told Newsweek why some men don't pay:

"If they have grown distant from their children, fathers come to view child support like making payments on a car they no longer own. Child support becomes a debt competing with all others."

SEXUAL JEALOUSY

Jealousy may prompt a father to refuse to make payments when his ex-wife lets a boyfriend move in with her and the children. He resents the man having sex with his former mate while he feels he is subsidizing them. Even if the woman is merely dating another man, the father often seeks revenge by not paying.

Sometimes fathers refuse to cooperate with support orders because they feel they have been unjustly treated by the courts or their ex-spouses. Because money is thought of as power, many fathers don't pay support as a way of exercising control over their former households.

Dads aren't the only deadbeats. Moms can be equally irresponsible in ignoring their children's financial needs when the father gets custody. The number of deadbeat moms is variously estimated at 5 to 10 percent of all non-paying parents.

Newsweek cited the case of a woman who owed her ex-husband more than $70,000 in support payments for their four children.

"She could never understand that I was paying the light and gas and the rent and child care," said the former husband, an assistant university professor. The mother said she had been devastated over losing custody and she couldn't pay because she was a full-time student. She said she later got a good-paying job and began giving the children thousands of dollars worth of gifts.

SOME DADS SIMPLY CAN'T PAY

Most men can pay more in child support than they are required to, studies show. But there are many fathers who simply cannot afford it, because they either are unemployed or earn so little.

These fathers seldom fit the stereotype of the deadbeat dad who enjoys an affluent lifestyle while their former families struggle to get by. Many are poorly educated, lack job skills, or can't work because they are ill or disabled. Their work history may be so erratic that they can't qualify for jobs that pay enough to support themselves and their children. Frequently, they need help in finding work.

These fathers find the child support orders so inflexible they can't begin to comply. Whether a father is working or not, a support order requires him to pay. They wind up owing thousands of dollars and may face jail for nonpayment. Some disappear, or work in jobs where their wages can't be garnished because they are paid in cash.

Dr. Jean Bonhomme, of the Atlanta-based National Black Men's Health Network, told a federal panel that some fathers were being unfairly castigated and viewed as criminals.

"If we look at why men don't pay support, they may not be the ogres they are made out to be," Bonhomme told the panel. "They may have employment problems or health problems. We feel willful non-payment of child support should be a crime, but a lack of job skills should not be."

Some experimental programs, with federal and private financing, have been started in various states to help unemployed fathers find jobs so they can support their children who are on welfare.

NATIONAL STATISTICS

- Two-thirds of all poor families with children are headed by single parents.
- 10 million women are raising children without a father in the home. They include about 3 million mothers who never married, 3 million who are divorced, and nearly 4 million still married or separated.
- 16 million children are living in homes without fathers.
- One of every four children is born to an unwed mother.
- Teenage mothers account for nearly one third of all out-of-wedlock births.

Source: CSE report citing statistics published by the U.S. Bureau of the Census. Figures largely based on 1990 data.

She Tracked Down Deadbeat Husband 15 Years After He Abandoned Three Kids

Pat Bennett's 15-year struggle to collect child support for her children was so remarkable that a book was written about it, followed by a made-for-television movie. She also told her story at a congressional subcommittee hearing on deadbeat parents who cross state lines to avoid paying child support.

Bennett

Her marriage to a former Marine had turned sour. A Virginia court awarded her $50 a week in support for her daughters, ages 1 and 2. She was pregnant again. But her husband, who had been a debt collector, disappeared in 1969 after paying her less than $100. "I was forced to go on public assistance from which I received $220 a month," she testified.

The runaway dad was determined not to see his family again. But he couldn't guess how determined she would be to find him. Pat Bennett, who later divorced him, found that governmental agencies were of no help in tracking him for the child support he owed.

She told the House subcommittee that he took on "a complete new identity, actually taking the name, Social Security number, and educational credentials of another person." The FBI and federal prosecutors refused to pursue an indictment because "they did not feel that my ex-husband was really a criminal....(they) were very, very wrong," she testified.

"The only way to make some fathers take their support obligations seriously is to threaten them with jail," she added.

At the start, Bennett knew she wasn't ready emotionally to find him on her own. She got some financial help from her parents but had to stay on welfare for two years. The experience humiliated her. Having no job training, she returned to college and began taking college courses in business and accounting.

She toughed it out, graduated and got a job with the Internal

Revenue Service. She became an IRS agent in Washington. She would later get a master's degree in business administration and a law degree.

She didn't know where her ex-husband had gone but was angry that he had deliberately evaded helping to support his three children. At one point, his foster parents had him legally declared dead. Bennett applied to Social Security for death benefits for her children, but the request was rejected.

She began her search. She learned he was using a different name and was in Texas, where he had been working in insurance. She got information over the telephone from personnel departments and government clerks. She traced him to Florida, where she heard he was again working in insurance. Then she began checking insurance regulators there to see if he was registered. He was, under the assumed name.

"I was not willing to let my ex-husband shed his family so easily," she testified. "I searched for him for 15 years before finding him in Tampa, Fla., in 1984."

She criticized Virginia officials for refusing to ask that her ex-husband be extradited from Florida on charges of non-support and desertion. She took a Virginia judgment for $106,000 to a Florida court, but her ex-husband refused to pay it. In 1987, a Florida court refused to hold him in criminal contempt.

Outraged, she filed an appeal and won. But then he appealed to the Florida Supreme Court. Financially strapped, she wrote her own brief and argued her own case. She won, and began getting $100 a week in child support — 23 years after he had walked out.

"At this rate, (he) will pay off the arrearage in 30 years — a bargain for the man who stole the childhood from his own three children," she told the congressional subcommittee.

Bennett now practices family law in Springfield, Va.

3

DADS CHALLENGE DEADBEAT STIGMA

Many fathers who love and support their children say they are being unfairly tarnished because they are absent fathers. They say they share the stigma of those society brands as deadbeat dads.

CONFLICTS OVER VISITATION, CUSTODY HURT KIDS

Some say their ex-spouses take their support money but deny them visitation and alienate the children from them. Even though they have a legal order for visitation, they say, the courts ignore their plight.

One father, who said he had paid child support regularly, wrote a letter to his local newspaper to complain bitterly that he had been denied visitation rights by his ex-wife.

"The only provisions in my court orders that are enforceable are those that relate to the payment of money," he wrote. "It is wrong that an estranged father who loves his children has no effective method to enforce visitation, communication and his love for his children."

Fathers' rights groups and others in the child support arena avoid using the term "Deadbeat Dad," saying it is unfair to men and sets the stage for sexist conflict.

Instead, they use expressions such as deadbeat parents, non-custodial parent, non-paying parent, non-resident, absent father or obligor.

OUR DEFINITION OF A DEADBEAT

We use the term Deadbeat Dad to describe a father who can afford to pay child support but won't.

We don't apologize for calling fathers deadbeats for abandoning their children financially and emotionally. It so happens that about 90 percent of deadbeat parents are men. (One census report showed nearly nine of every ten custodial parents are women).

Some parents who owe support can't pay it because they may be unemployed, working for low wages or unemployable for some reason.

But working fathers, and even mothers, who purposely shirk their duty should be ashamed to go bed each night without first assuring that their children have adequate food, clothing, shelter and care that day. Calling such a person a deadbeat may be too charitable. Jerk would be better.

LET'S NOT KEEP DADS FROM KIDS

We agree with many men who complain it's unfair for a mother to get child support and deny the father visitation rights. If judges can enforce court-ordered support payments, they should also enforce visitation rights spelled out in court orders. How can a father be a real father without seeing his children?

A mother who hurts her kids by keeping them from having contact with their father is also a jerk.

The courts or other agencies should intervene and get the mother to cooperate in letting the father see his kids. Mediation programs are being used in many areas to ensure visitation. This also helps in keeping the absent parent from stopping payments out of anger.

Attorney Jeffery Leving, author of a book on fathers' rights, suggests temporarily abating the child support, or putting the money in a trust, until visitation is restored. But this may hurt the children.

Most of the state child support officials we surveyed responded with a firm "no" when asked if paying support and visitation should be linked. They said these are separate issues and their agencies can't get into such disputes. Some said visitation is an emotional issue and they would lack resources to deal with it.

While it's unfair for fathers to be denied visitation by spiteful moms, it's just as wrong for dads to use that as an excuse for not paying support. Fathers should continue to support their children, while pressing their right to court-ordered visitation.

FATHERS' RIGHTS GROUPS GROWING

In recent years, there has been a growing number of fathers' rights groups campaigning for better treatment for men in cases involving child support, custody and visitation.

Many serve as self-help groups and refer members to lawyers and other resources. Leaders in the movement seek public forums, testify for reforms before legislative committees, write letters to newspapers and organize local chapters of frustrated and angry fathers.

Their issues include granting custody to the father, greater use of joint custody, lowering child support awards, ending gender-bias in favor of women, assuring more fairness in the courts, promoting the role of the father in the child's development, and enforcing children's rights of access to both parents and grandparents.

Ronald K. Henry, an attorney speaking for a group called Children's Rights Council, told a congressional subcommittee that it's wrong to label some fathers as deadbeats when their only crime is not being able to pay. He called for "child support orders that are in accordance with true ability to pay."

"The popular stereotype of the 'deadbeat' is the guy in the Mercedes who abandoned his children. The reality is that most delinquent [fathers] are economically marginal," he said.

"Demonization of non-custodial parents is used to justify all manner of inhumane treatment," including jailing them, Henry said. He said this violates a constitutional prohibition against putting debtors in prison.

DADS SCORNED AS "WALKING CASH REGISTERS"

David L. Levy, speaking as president of the Children's Rights Council, was quoted: "Deadbeat parents are on everybody's lips.... but pushed-away or forced-away parents are not. They've been regarded as absentee parents, walking cash registers who are told, 'Send a check or otherwise get lost.' "

Levy says child support and visitation are linked and should not be treated as separate issues. The council supports conciliation and mediation to reduce hostilities in family breakups so the children can have access to both parents.

SOME WARY OF FATHERS' GROUPS

Despite the stated goals of dozens of fathers' rights groups, they pose a serious threat to child support reform efforts, says **Barbara Grob,** director of the San Francisco-based Child Support Reform Initiative.

She said they argue that child-support awards are too high. "They aim to redefine men as a highly-aggrieved, disempowered group in society.... it has clear implications for the well-being of children," she said.

Grob says while some dads can't pay, that shouldn't "obscure a larger truth: that most of the men who do not make child support payments can afford to pay."

Henry, the attorney with the Children's Rights Council, says: "Social science research [has] confirmed that the best parent is both parents ....children need two parents."

WHAT'S BEST FOR THE KIDS

In this war of words, many on both sides agree that stigmatizing some fathers as deadbeat dads in an attempt to shame them into paying can be harmful to the children, who may be stigmatized themselves.

Grob, of the Child Support Reform Initiative, feels that relying on public embarrassment works only temporarily. To get beyond warring parents, the focus should be to give child support national priority as a children's issue, she says.

Grob favors a campaign, such as the one against drunk driving, that would send this message: "It is not acceptable to turn our backs on children." The routine payment of child support should become a responsibility that all parents are expected to meet, rather than an adversarial issue, she said.

MANY CHILDREN NEVER KNOW WHAT A FATHER IS

Syndicated columnist William Raspberry says the importance of fathers has been downgraded and this is causing any number of America's social crises, including crime and violence. "Boys who grow up without fathers are less likely to get the discipline that can keep them straight," he wrote. He says the decline in the importance of marriage makes boys and men less valuable to their families and communities.

Raspberry

Raspberry, in reviewing **David Blankenhorn's** book, *Fatherless America,* agrees that the nation's most urgent social problem is having so many children abandoned by their fathers. They never know what it means to have a father.

Blankenhorn says the trend toward fatherlessness has become rooted in the culture and must be reversed. He told Raspberry:

"We are talking about how to get a huge number of [fathers] to change their minds.... it's very hard to figure out.... The people who say we can't do anything about the trend may be right. Nobody knows. I do know that we'll never change the culture if we just sit around and say we can't."

David Levy Hates The Deadbeat Label

"It sends a negative message to kids," David L. Levy says. "Fathers should be seen as participants in the raising of their children."

Levy

Levy is president of the Children's Rights Council, a group in Washington, D.C. that campaigns for father's rights and fair financial child support. One goal is to preserve a child's contact with both parents.

Levy says when the child support issue is debated it's usually about financial support. He prefers to talk about "emotional support" which he says children need from both parents.

ADVICE TO MOMS

His advice to mothers who would keep their children from contact with their father:

"Separate your needs from your child's needs. You may want to ex your ex out of your life. But the child deserves the love and joy of both parents. That child needs both of you. Respect the parenting ability of the other parent. The child will ultimately be thankful."

Levy said he was in a year-long custody battle with his first wife, who had custody of their son. He said she had left the state but then came back and he got more access to his son. "It sensitized me," he said.

He got involved with others who were concerned with the father's role and rights after a divorce and helped found the Children's Rights Council in 1985.

The council has chapters in 32 states and most of its members are men. It campaigns for fairness in divorce situations, including such issues as custody, visitation and child support.

"I have never seen this as men versus women," he said, noting that the council also speaks for visitation rights of non-custodial moms.

Some child support activists are wary of the council's goals, saying it opposed child support reform measures and supported efforts to reduce child support obligations of non-custodial parents.

Levy defends the council's positions saying it also supported changes it believes would increase support collections.

He likes to cite studies that back his views, such as one showing parents with access to their children paying child support at twice the rate as those who don't have access.

"The children are the main victims" in hostilities between warring parents, he said. "Instead of rewarding spitefulness, you reward cooperation. You show both parents have the same rights. The incentive for fighting would be removed."

The council backs programs that require divorcing parents to go through a conciliation session that stresses the hardship a divorce can have on the children.

"GET THE CHIP OFF"

"It helps the parents get the chip off their shoulders.... it's preventative and cuts down on disputes later," he said. Mediation programs are also helpful in post-divorce situations involving visitation disputes, he said.

Levy has no objection to having the IRS take over child support collections, "if they'll enforce visitation rights." He said maybe there could be financial penalties on violators of visitation requirements.

Levy, who was a government copyright lawyer, retired after working 27 years at the Library of Congress. His work with the council is a full-time pursuit.

"It takes a lot of time. I wish we weren't needed, but we are, repairing families. The family structure is key to so many problems."

4

HOW IT'S SUPPOSED TO WORK

Congress would never have created the massive child support enforcement system we now have if family breadwinners, even when they left the home, did the right thing and supported their kids.

THE GOVERNMENT AS COLLECTOR

The breakup of families over the last three decades and the shirking of responsibility by so many fathers caused Congress to take steps to protect the children. It mandated state and local governments to become the collector of child support payments, with the federal government setting the standards and paying the major share — more than 80 percent — of the collection costs.

Unfortunately, much of the support money goes uncollected. The reasons include:

• Fathers who refuse to pay.

• Failure to establish paternity.

• Bulging caseloads and inept collection efforts by state and local agencies.

• Mothers who are unable to get child support and accept defeat.

For all its faults, mothers must deal with this inefficient system. It's the vehicle you must use, whether you are divorced, separated or never married to the father.

Child Support Enforcement (CSE) agencies vary from state to state. They are required to locate non-custodial parents, establish paternity, obtain support orders, enforce them, and collect the child-support payments. The agencies work with prosecutors, and other law enforcement agencies, and family or domestic relations courts.

In divorce cases, the mother may have reached agreement about the monthly amount of child support, with the court ordering the payment. An unmarried mother must establish paternity before getting a court order.

To apply for child support, contact your local Child Support Enforcement office. It should appear in your telephone directory under the county or state listings.

Any parent or person with custody of a child can apply for child support or medical support — whether they're on welfare or not.

If you are on welfare, you will receive up to $50 of any support payment collected, with the state getting the rest as repayment for the welfare checks.

In non-welfare cases, child support payments collected by the state are sent to the families. The state must charge an application fee of up to $25, but may pay the fee from its own funds. Some states may seek to recover part of their costs by deducting from the support payments or by billing the non-custodial parent.

THE FOUR KEY STEPS

The process involves four stages: Locating the father, establishing paternity, getting the support order and collecting the child support. Let's explore each.

1. FINDING THE FATHER

You should know — or find out — where he lives and works. The CSE agency needs a correct address in order to notify him that a legal claim for support is being made. The caseworker is required to help you locate him, just as you must try to help the state find him. In some cases, a mother seeking welfare who fears the father might harm her or the children may not be required to identify or help find him.

You should supply his Social Security number and the name of his employer, if you know it. Also helpful will be names, addresses and phone numbers of relatives, friends, past employers or others who might help find him. If you don't know his Social Security number, furnishing his date and place of birth, or his parents' names, would be helpful. In later chapters, we will go into detail about gathering this type of information

If he can't be found locally, your CSE office will ask the State Parent Locator Service to check other state agency records, such as income tax and motor vehicle registrations. If it appears he moved to another state, then the office can ask the other state and the Federal Parent Locator Service to search records of various agencies for a current address.

The federal checks can include computerized records of the Internal Revenue Service, Social Security, military and veterans records and state employment agencies.

2. ESTABLISHING PATERNITY

Millions of children are on welfare because their mothers haven't proved paternity.

You can't get a child support order without establishing paternity. If you never married, the father must admit parenthood or be proven to be the father. Even when he acknowledges it, in some states you may still have to go to court to establish legal fatherhood. If he refuses to admit it, genetic or blood testing can be ordered.

Unwed fathers are more apt to acknowledge their paternity at the birthing hospital and go along with a request by the hospital staff to co-sign an affidavit with the mother. Some states make this equivalent to proof of paternity, while others allow the affidavit to be used as evidence in court to determine legal fatherhood.

Your caseworker needs your help in proving paternity. You should provide as much information as you can about the father, your relationship with him and details about your pregnancy and the birth of your child.

If there is uncertainty on the part of either the man or the mother, or if he denies paternity, the court can order genetic tests or highly accurate tests of blood samples of the man, mother and child. When more than one man could be the father, each may be required to undergo testing.

A father can't escape paternity just by running away. If he fails to respond to a formal complaint served on him, a default judgment can be entered in court establishing paternity. A support order can then be issued.

Establishing paternity is important in other ways. It is the child's passport to getting health and life insurance benefits, as well as Social Security death benefits or veterans benefits if the father dies.

John Dockery, an assistant prosecutor in St. Louis, put it this way:

"Sometime in the next 18 years, the father is going to get a job, or die. If he gets a job, the kid gets money. If he dies, the kid gets Social Security."

In Los Angeles, an unmarried mother and her young daughter were on welfare. A state caseworker helped the mother establish paternity. Later, the father won a large lottery jackpot. The child then began getting more than $2,000 a month in child support.

Similar cases involve college athletes who go on to make millions playing on professional teams. One standout basketball player admitted paternity but said he didn't have money to pay child support. That all changed when he signed an NBA contract for $2.5 million. Attorneys then began negotiating a settlement for his son.

If the father is in the military he can draw an extra allowance for the child as a dependent. The child would also be eligible for commissary and post exchange privileges, as well as military health and insurance benefits. If the father suffers a service-related disability, the child could qualify for educational benefits.

Paternity gives the child born out of wedlock the same rights as the child whose parents are married, including qualifying as an heir in estate proceedings. It allows children to know their family and medical history. Early detection and prevention of disease may depend on knowledge of the child's family history.

On an emotional level, the child may benefit from knowing who the father is. The child's self-esteem may flourish from having a chance to bond with the father and getting to know his side of the family tree, as well as experiencing the kinship of paternal grandparents.

When paternity is established early, the better it is for the child. There is less chance for the father to estrange himself and less time for the mother to distance herself and the child from the father.

3. GETTING THE SUPPORT ORDER

After the father is located and paternity is established, the next step is getting a legal order for child support that spells out the monthly amount due and how it is to be paid.

The caseworker or mother's lawyer may discuss the child's financial needs with both parents and review their finances and the father's ability to pay. Each state is required to have guidelines for setting the level of support from the father. But the guidelines vary from state to state, and children are often punished in states that set low awards.

Some guidelines include costs for medical insurance and for day-care. To estimate the amount of support your child may be entitled to, obtain from your local court clerk or CSE office a copy of your state's guidelines.

Setting the amount of child support is not always done by a judge. Many states use administrative procedures and legal hearings to speed up the process. Such hearings may be conducted by a master or referee of the court or an administrative hearing officer. If the parents agree on the amount of child support and the payment schedule, they can sign an agreement which can be legally binding when approved by the court or the hearing officer. Often, the court may include the terms of custody and visitation. In cases where the father is less than open about his income, the caseworker must make every effort to identify his employment, income and assets. This can be done by subpoenaing the father's earnings records from an employer or tax returns.

If the father is self-employed, works for cash, or lives in another state, he may be able to hide his income. (In a later chapter we'll discuss how to uncover hidden income and assets.)

By the same token, you as the mother, must disclose your income and what you own.

At some point, you may have defend your figures if the father alleges that you are understating your income. If the father remarries and is responsible for a second family, or has another child support order, he may be able to get the amount of your support order reduced.

By law, issues such as visitation and custody are not within the scope of the Child Support Enforcement program. Parents must deal with them through the local court system. Check with your caseworker, or attorney, to find out about your state's laws and resources which may address custody and visitation.

In a divorce case, each parent is required to list all income, property and other assets and debts, whether jointly or individual. Each also must list his or her living expenses and other obligations. Both sides and their lawyers often jockey for the most favorable reading. If the couple is unable to agree to on a figure, the court makes its own decision and issues an order for the monthly amount to be paid.

4. ENFORCING THE SUPPORT ORDER

The support order is of little good unless you can regularly collect the amount due. Millions of mothers have found this out, when the father refuses to pay or can't pay. To make ends meet, mothers often apply for welfare.

Usually, support payments are paid into the court system and the money is then forwarded to the mother. This creates a record of payments.

The best situation is when child support payments are made by wage withholding through the father's employer. Several years ago, Congress mandated that immediate wage withholding be included in all court orders. An exception can be made if both parents agree to an alternate payment plan. States are suppose to honor and continue wage withholding orders from other states.

Federal law requires employers to cooperate in withholding, but some fail to do it because they are unaware of the law.

If they choose, states can withhold other income as well, such as commissions, bonuses, retirement, rental, interest and even unemployment benefits. In cases where fathers ignore support orders or are in arrears, states can seize their state or federal income tax refunds. They can also put liens on real or personal property owned by the father, thus preventing him from selling the property or borrowing against it, without first paying the child support debt. The state may be able to seize and sell his property, with the proceeds applied to his support debt.

A mother can have her own attorney work to collect support payments through wage withholding. Or the attorney can work through the Child Support Enforcement program to coordinate collection efforts.

In theory, deadbeat dads can't avoid their obligations to support their children by fleeing to other states. Many states have an array of weapons that can be used to pressure deadbeat dads. These include filing garnishments, asking the IRS to determine the dad's income and assets and to intercept tax refunds, reporting delinquent fathers to credit bureaus, and publicizing the names of some of the more flagrant deadbeats.

Under federal law, states are required to work with each other to establish and enforce support orders. They are supposed to work just as hard for the benefit of children in other states as they would in their own jurisdiction. All states have passed some form of the Uniform Reciprocal Enforcement of Support Act (URESA). The basic mechanism is a two-state lawsuit to locate the father, establish paternity, obtain a support order and collect on it.

But each state is self-governing, with an independent court system with differing laws and practices. For mothers pursuing runaway dads, the interstate cases are the most frustrating because of lack of cooperation among the states, insufficient resources, poor tracking of cases, and bureaucratic indifference — as you'll see in the next chapter.

A new law has been adopted by Congress to replace the often unwieldy URESA provisions in interstate cases. It was passed as part of the Welfare Reform Bill. It's called the Uniform Interstate Family Support Act (UIFSA). Congress directed states to adopt provisions of the newer law for interstate cases by January 1998. Some states didn't meet the deadline.

Get This Valuable Handbook

The federal Office of Child Support Enforcement publishes an excellent free guide on how the system works. It's called "Handbook On Child Support Enforcement."

Ask your caseworker for a copy. Or you can request a copy by calling the Office of Child Support Enforcement at (202) 401-9383 or writing to:

Office of Child Support Enforcement
National Reference Center
370 L'Enfant Promenade, SW
Washington, DC 20447

THE CHILD SUPPORT LAWS

Since the early 1950s, Congress has shown a continued interest in child support. But not until 1975 — after the divorce rate soared — did it take a major step, requiring the states to join in tackling the non-support problem.

That year, Congress amended the Social Security Act to set up the Child Support Enforcement program, known as Title IV-D (Four-D). This created a federal-state effort with the feds setting the standards and paying a good chunk of the cost.

Through the Office of Child Support Enforcement, the federal government oversees the state-based system and imposes regulations that govern what states must do to comply with federal laws.

States that don't comply risk losing federal funding for their welfare and child support programs.

Changes in the enforcement program, enacted in 1984, allow the states to garnish wages, attach bank accounts, intercept income-tax refunds and put liens on real estate to recover delinquent child support.

The 1984 changes by Congress required local governments to help any custodial parent, not just the poor, to collect child support. Newsweek called it a little-noticed revolution — "one of the most sweeping pieces of social legislation in decades."

But to many mothers, its promises have yet to be fulfilled. On average, the states report collecting child support in only about 19 per cent of their cases.

In 1988, Congress created the U. S. Commission on Interstate Child Support, as part of the Family Support Act. The Commission is charged with proposing to Congress changes to improve establishing and enforcing child support awards across state lines.

In 1992, Congress made it a federal crime to willfully avoid paying child support by moving from one state to another. It also required credit reporting agencies to include child support debts on a person's credit report.

In 1994, the Bankruptcy Reform Act provided that child support debt could not be discharged in bankruptcy. And it assigned child support a priority claim in collecting from debtors.

In 1996, as part of welfare overhaul, Congress and the executive branch pushed through enforcement measures to crack down on non-paying parents. Included was a national directory of new hires (reported by employers) to track delinquent parents across state lines.

U.S. Rep. Lynn Woolsey Becomes A Voice for Reform

When the subject is reform of the child support system and the speaker is Lynn Woolsey, people listen.

Woolsey

She's been there, having raised three kids without child support from her ex-husband. While in her late 20's she had to go on welfare for three years.

We're talking about Congresswoman Lynn Woolsey, a Democrat representing Marin County and most of Sonoma County, both north of San Francisco. She's co-sponsor of legislation to revamp the child support collection system.

Her experience as a young mom who had to struggle to make ends meet has given her the insight to understand the child support problem. And a certain wisdom in proposing remedies to improve collections.

Before there was a child support enforcement program she had to apply for general assistance even while she was working to support her children. Her ex-husband, a stockbroker, had left the state. Said Woolsey:

"I had been living a 'Leave It To Beaver' life — successful husband, beautiful home, healthy kids — and suddenly through no fault of my own or my children's, I was left alone with no child support to raise my family. If the United States had a child support system like the one I have proposed, I might not have needed to go on welfare in the first place."

She had no house and no job skills. She had to fib about her circumstances to land her first job. She supplemented her wages with ADC payments for food stamps, Medicaid and child care assistance.

She remarried and left the assistance rolls. She did secretarial work, worked as a human resources manager for a large firm, got a college degree and ran her own consulting and employment agency. She served on the Petaluma, Calif., city council and in 1992 was elected to Congress.

During the debate on welfare reform Woolsey relied on her life experience to argue that people moving from welfare to work needed assistance.

She spoke again from experience when she and Rep. Henry J. Hyde, a Republican from Illinois, proposed legislation to have the IRS collect and distribute child support payments.

A STRANGE UNION

Woolsey, a liberal Democrat, told the authors it was a "strange union" when she teamed up with Hyde, a conservative Republican who is highly respected in Congress. They pushed to attach their child support changes to welfare reform legislation. But it didn't succeed.

Woolsey said she and Hyde came at the child support issue from different angles. "It's not a liberal or conservative issue. It's right or wrong — you don't abandon your children."

They came back with a bill to have the IRS collect child support and send the checks to the custodial parent. The Woolsey-Hyde measure required that employers deduct child support from paychecks, just like taxes and Social Security. Compliance would be enforced by the IRS.

"We figure over 500,000 kids would be off welfare immediately," Woolsey said.

She cited a General Accounting Office report that said since 1985 the states have been collecting child support in only about 20 percent of their caseloads.

"The states have had their chance to improve child support collection, but they have failed our children and bankrupted our welfare system....It is a national crisis demanding a national solution," she said.

While their bill got stalled, Woolsey said there is bi-partisan support for the revamping of the collection system, although some in Congress are not fond of the IRS.

In the Senate, bills with goals similar to the Hyde/Woolsey measure were sponsored by Sen. Christopher J. Dodd, D-Conn., and Sen. John F. Kerry, D-Mass.

Woolsey says the current system allows states and counties to ignore the mom who is owed child support and is barely making ends meet, but is not yet on welfare. "The system has nothing invested in helping her. We've got to prevent mothers like her her from going on welfare."

The media should do better in helping the public understand the child support problem, she said, adding: "They (media) make people think it's the fault of the moms and children when they go on welfare."

DON'T PIT KIDS AGAINST DADS

Woolsey is concerned about protecting visitation rights for fathers, saying the courts should enforce these rights along with the child support order.

"I never prevented my children from seeing their father, even though I never got anything," she said. She urges single moms not to use the children against their father. "It's too hard on the kids. No matter how tempting, don't do it."

She believes too many men have the wrong attitude about avoiding child support. "Peer pressure would help. Maybe you won't change their minds. But the important thing is to collect the child support to help the kids. The sons shouldn't grow up thinking it's right" to be a deadbeat.

She says some of the existing collection agencies and child support officials "think the effort to have the IRS do the collecting will hurt their job security." She says it really won't because they will still be part of setting the awards and handling the cases. It's just that the collection would be done differently, and a whole lot better."

She advises women pursuing their child support not to give up. "Keep pushing and pushing, because it's owed, it's deserved," she says.

Also, she says moms should get involved with grassroots groups, such as ACES. "If you can't find one, start one. It helps to know you are not alone and can change the situation with some help."

5

THE SYSTEM'S A MESS

In most states the child support collection system is in disarray — despite billions spent for federal and state administrative costs. For the five-year period ending in 1995, about $11.6 billion was spent.

And for what? Still, only one in five families gets help.

Those working in the system find themselves burdened with too many cases and unable to mesh their efforts with other agencies. Some may play favorites in choosing who they are going to help. Many mothers seeking help for their children feel they have been abandoned once again, this time by the system.

Truth is, it has rarely worked well. While more than $10 billion in child support is collected each year across the nation, more than four times that amount remains uncollected, most of it piling up from prior years. These figures are from annual reports to Congress by the federal Office of Child Support Enforcement.

In recent years, collections have been made in only about 19 percent of the child support cases nationally — less than one in each five cases.

A Census Bureau study showed that 44 percent of single women with children whose father was absent never got a child support order. Of those who did, one fourth got no support money, another fourth received partial payments, and about half got the full amount due.

DEADBEATS HEAD FOR THE BORDER

It has become a highway ritual. Fathers bent on deserting their children get out their maps and hit the road. Many wind up in other states, safe from having to pay their child support.

Margaret Campbell Haynes headed The U.S. Commission on Interstate Child Support, which investigated problems across the nation. She deplores the fact that so many deadbeat fathers get away without paying.

"Three quarters of custodial mothers entitled to child support either lack child support orders or do not receive full payment under such orders. In no other area of financial responsibility does this country tolerate such an abysmal record," Haynes declared.

AMONG THE PANEL'S FINDINGS:

• Children in families where the parents live in different states suffer the most, financially and emotionally. Nearly one-third of child support cases are interstate. Yet, only $1 of every $10 collected is from an interstate case.

• Interstate collections are beset by lack of cooperation and communication among the states and their bureaucracies, antiquated case tracking systems, insufficient resources, and inadequate training of caseworkers, attorneys and judges.

• Broad reforms are needed. The system is plagued by a bewildering maze of different state laws, policies and procedures. There are difficulties in locating and serving legal papers on the parent who owes support.

The problems that the commission cited several years ago exist still. A later study by the Government Accounting Office found that children in interstate cases are twice as likely to get nothing than children whose fathers live in the same state.

Many dads on the run ignore court orders issued in their former home states. State boundaries are an inherent barrier to an efficient and uniform collection system. The states often don't share quickly enough information about a deadbeat's income. One state may not learn that a support order had been issued in another state until it is too late and the father has disappeared.

Even when courts try to be fair to all concerned, the playing field is not always level. One domestic relations official in Pennsylvania explained it this way:

"When you file an action from one state to another, you're at an immediate disadvantage because the party you're trying to get support from is the only one standing there in front of the judge. It's a lot easier for the judge to be more sympathetic to the person in front of him than the person he will never see and only knows from the paper in front of him.

"There is a district attorney or some sort of legal counsel supposed to be there representing the plaintiff from the other state, but more often than not this person is either new, doesn't understand, or doesn't know what is going on."

BROKAW: COMPUTERS GONE HAYWIRE

TV Anchorman Tom Brokaw reported on one big problem: Computer systems to help the states talk with each other and track child support cases are goofed up.

Brokaw, on an NBC "Fleecing of America" expose, said the computer hookup was a costly failure. Despite getting more than $2 billion from the federal government for computers, 43 states failed to meet the federal guidelines. Many of the states' computers simply couldn't talk to each other, according to the report.

"Deadbeat dads are getting help from the fouled up computer system," Brokaw said, calling it "a good idea gone haywire." He cited a report by ACES, the Association for Children for Enforcement of Support, which found that many child support files are outdated and inaccurate.

California spent $100 million on a computer system to track deadbeats. It was so fraught with problems that the governor pulled the plug. The state was already behind on meeting its deadline when the meltdown occurred.

A BUNCH OF FLUNK OUTS

If they were graded, most of the states would get poor or failing marks. Nationwide, states on average collect child support in only 19 percent of their cases, as the chart in this chapter shows. In 1995, support was collected in only 3.7 million cases out of a total caseload of 18.9 million. A state can claim a collection even in a case where only a few dollars are collected during the year.

Indiana ranked lowest on the chart, collecting support in only 9.8 percent of its cases during the year. Others at the bottom included: Washington, D.C. — 10.5 percent; Illinois — 10.8; Tennessee — 11.2; Arizona — 11.7; Wyoming — 12.2; Rhode Island — 12.6; and Mississippi — 12.7.

HOW STATES RANK IN COLLECTIONS

1995 Rank	State	Caseload	Cases with Collection	Collections Percentages
1	Minn.	225,696	91,247	40.4
2	Wis.	411,085	157,555	38.8
3	Va.	363,058	136,411	37.6
4	Maine	75,898	27,034	35.6
5	N.H.	44,494	15,673	35.2
6	Vt.	19,336	6,731	34.8
7	Kan.	129,458	44,210	34.2
8	Wash.	360,317	120,051	33.3
9	S.D.	30,479	9,993	32.8
10	Pa.	882,374	271,496	30.8
11	Idaho	62,194	18,196	29.3
12	Ohio	906,266	253,432	28.0
13	Del.	55,541	15,513	27.9
14	Mass.	218,126	58,375	26.8
15	S.C.	218,243	56,820	26.0
16	Ark.	130,332	33,784	25.9
17	N.D.	37,357	9,355	25.0
18	Hawaii	52,748	13,157	24.9
19	W.Va.	117,204	28,453	24.3
20	N.J.	536,610	129,161	24.1
21	Md.	362,345	83,258	23.0
22	N.C.	442,765	97,664	22.1
23	Nev.	74,311	16,098	21.7
24	Iowa	182,669	39,173	21.4
25	Ala.	371,071	78,718	21.2
26	Mont.	43,781	9,034	20.6
27	Utah	110,092	21,479	19.5
28	Texas	736,413	143,174	19.4
29	Ore.	253,447	48,806	19.3
30	Neb.	138,878	26,515	19.1
31	Ga.	515,830	97,351	18.9
32	Mo.	375,299	69,092	18.4
33	Okla.	118,132	21,715	18.4
34	Alaska	53,350	9,147	17.1
35	Ky.	305,178	50,157	16.4
36	Conn.	227,221	36,884	16.2
37	N.M.	92,570	14,713	15.9
38	Fla.	1,020,738	160,766	15.7
39	Mich.	1,508,480	232,564	15.4
40	N.Y.	1,282,835	192,935	15.0
41	Colo.	195,336	29,305	15.0
42	Calif.	2,367,404	328,691	13.9
43	La.	366,600	49,420	13.5
44	Miss.	285,662	36,391	12.7
45	R.I.	77,801	9,810	12.6
46	Wyo.	46,294	5,642	12.2
47	Ariz.	285,123	33,255	11.7
48	Tenn.	622,292	69,794	11.2
49	Ill.	721,151	77,926	10.8
50	D.C.	93,304	9,801	10.5
51	Ind.	777,706	76,308	9.8
		18,930,894	3,672,233	19.4

Source: Office of Child Support Enforcement

Minnesota had the best rate, collecting in 40.4 percent of its cases. Others at the top included: Wisconsin — 38.8 percent; Virginia — 37.6; Maine — 35.6; New Hampshire — 35.2; Vermont — 34.8; Kansas — 34.2; and Washington state— 33.3.

Newspaper reports in recent years depict how some states are having problems or failing children who are owed child support. Here's a sampling:

ILLINOIS: The St. Louis Post-Dispatch found the Illinois collection effort to be appalling. Its series cited a state audit that showed $1.3 billion in support had gone uncollected over a 20-year period. Collection duties were fragmented among a dozen public and private agencies. Much of the debt was so old that the money would never find its way to the children who needed it.

"Illinois has such a bad reputation for collecting support that child-support workers around the country refer to it as 'the black hole.' Cases go in but payments don't come out," the paper said.

MINNESOTA: Despite having a collection rate that other states would envy, the **St. Paul Pioneer Press** didn't mince words in summing up findings of a six-month investigation it made several years ago: "Minnesota's children are being robbed of millions of dollars every year by deadbeat parents and a system of judges, social workers, prosecutors, lawmakers and welfare officials unwilling or unable to do anything about it."

"....The state's child support collection system has broken down, plunging thousands of families into a grim existence likely to be marked by poverty, poor health and crime," the paper said. It told how state law had shielded the identities of deadbeats, even those owing more than $50,000 in back support.

COLORADO: The Daily Sentinel, in Grand Junction, quoted critic Geraldine Jensen calling Colorado one of the worst states in collecting child support.

"It's a situation where over 90 percent of the children in need of payments don't receive payments and the government does nothing about it," she said. "It's an atrocity. It's causing children to go to bed hungry." Jensen is president of The Association For Children For Enforcement of Support (ACES).

CALIFORNIA: "Deadbeats Win, Kids Lose — Again." So read the headline of an editorial in the **Sacramento Bee.** The editorial, similar to those in other newspapers, cited a study which showed that county district attorneys were collecting in only 13 percent of their cases, putting California near the bottom of states for collecting child support.

The 1996 study, by legal aid and child advocacy groups, showed the state was collecting, on average, only $380 a year per family. Over 3.5 million children in the state got nothing, the study reported. Los Angeles County ranked next to last among the state's 58 counties. **The Los Angeles Times** said millions of deadbeat dads were getting off scot-free in California, owing $5 billion to their children. California has the highest number of child support cases in the nation.

ARIZONA: Mothers were so outraged at its dismal collection rate — 47th among states —that some of them sued the state for failing to help them get their support. One mom said she had been rebuffed 15 years earlier when a judge brushed off her child support request, hinting she was promiscuous, the **Associated Press** reported.

The woman and four others pursued their suit all the way to the U.S. Supreme Court. Their attorneys argued that Arizona violated their rights and they should be allowed to sue the state. The Clinton administration supported their position, but 42 states asked the high court to bar such suits. And it did, saying states cannot be sued to force compliance with federal efforts to collect child support. But the court said some suits might be allowed.

LAYING THE BLAME

Irwin Garfinkel, a scholar and expert on child support, says deadbeat dads should not get all the blame for the non-support mess.

Garfinkel

"Non-payment of child support may be attributable as much to ineffective government institutions as to fathers' reluctance to pay," the Columbia University professor said in a paper published with three other scholars in 1996.

"The judicial, legislative and executive branches of government are responsible for setting awards, making sure awards are adequate, and collecting what is owed," their paper said.

Garfinkel has written books about ways to assure support for children so they can avoid poverty. The published paper, entitled "Deadbeat Dads, Or Inept States?" makes these points:

• The nation's system of child support enforcement is essentially a collection of 51 different systems with each state largely setting its own policy and some states doing better than others. Some states make it easier to be a deadbeat dad because of their poor efforts at collecting.

• Child support awards are rarely updated to keep pace with inflation and payments vary substantially across the country.

• As child support reform continues, policymakers can learn from successful and even unsuccessful states. Ways must be found for measuring effective practices.

Garfinkel's view is echoed by others who have studied the problem.

A San Francisco-based advocacy group called **The Child Support Reform Initiative** says public officials like to claim that they're "getting tough with deadbeat dads."

But they rarely blame themselves or others involved in the collection system, the group said. "It is easier to simply lay the blame with individual 'deadbeat dads.'

"Failed state collection systems have significantly contributed to the explosion in unpaid child support. This fact is often missing from public debate. Most public officials are.... reluctant to criticize other public employees or to insist on real program accountability despite the billions invested in these flawed systems over the past 20 years.

"It is the ineffectual collection systems that allows so many parents to evade their obligation to make regular child support payments," the child advocacy group said.

IT'S NOT ALL BAD

Under pressure from Congress and the public, states are cracking down more on deadbeats. They have passed laws making it a felony to willfully avoid paying child support. And federal prosecutors have been prodded by the U.S. Attorney General to go after deadbeats who cross state lines to cheat their children.

More states are intercepting tax refunds, reporting deadbeats to credit bureaus across the country, stripping driving privileges, and yanking professional licenses. Some are hiring private collection agencies to track down the delinquents.

In various states, law officers over the years have come up with ploys to catch their man, including sting operations. In one Florida community, 70 persons wanted for various offenses — including deadbeat dads — showed up at a hotel ballroom after getting letters telling them they had won Super Bowl tickets. The only tickets they got were to jail.

In Kansas City, some deadbeats got letters offering them a chance at a $35-an-hour job and a free big-screen television set. They marched into a plush hotel ready to be interviewed. But instead they were snookered by authorities who had used the name of a bogus company on the letters. "They were told the big-screen TV was not available to them, because they were under arrest," an assistant prosecutor said.

Surprise raids also are being used. In New Jersey, teams of sheriff's deputies raided homes in 21 counties in a single day. By nightfall, they nabbed 457 people who owed more than $2 million in child support. In a Mother's Day raid, also in New Jersey, officers pulled in 432 deadbeat dads — and 10 deadbeat moms. One sheriff said Mother's Day seemed an appropriate time for the raids "to emphasize the depth of this problem and its ramifications."

Some states have borrowed an idea from the FBI's Most Wanted fliers, putting out their own lists of 10 Most Wanted child support deadbeats and the amounts they owe. The lists serve several purposes: they satisfy the public's outrage by publicly humiliating deadbeats; they generate tips from people who recognize the deadbeats and report their whereabouts; and they help force the dads to pay up so their families can get off welfare.

The lists and photos are posted in public places and released to the media. Some critics argue that public humiliation of a delinquent father can emotionally harm his child and this outweighs the value of the public listing.

Mom's Anguish With The System Gives Birth To Self-Help Group

Geraldine Jensen's life changed when a surly child-support official in Toledo berated her for demanding more help in getting support for her two sons.

Jensen

"I'm so tired of you women coming in here and whining and complaining," the man told her. "If you think you can do a better job, go do it."

She left infuriated. But later that day she used most of the $12 she had in her purse for a classified newspaper ad. It read: "Having problems collecting child support? Call me."

"People began to call and the phone hasn't stopped ringing," she said. The year was 1984. "Now we have the largest child-support organization in the nation."

It's called ACES — Association for Children for Enforcement of Support, Inc., a not-for-profit organization based in Toledo. Jensen is president of the self-help advocacy group that has grown to 35,000 members in more than 350 chapters.

She had been married at 18, had two children and then divorced. Her ex-spouse was ordered to pay $250 a month in child support. She went to work as a nurse's aide.

"He was paying child support and visiting the boys frequently," Jensen said. "That lasted for six months. Then the payments stopped and he also stopped visiting on a regular basis." He left town.

She was earning minimum wage and couldn't pay her bills. Her utilities were turned off, and the bank foreclosed on her home. Her boys were two and four. She and the children lived with her parents for a while, until she was able to rent her own apartment.

She applied for welfare, but was turned down because she was making too much money — $100 a week. A welfare worker advised her to quit her day job at a library to qualify for help. Instead, Jensen took a second job, selling household items during the evenings.

"MY SONS HAD NO PARENT"

One night, as she was about leave for work, her son Jake, then four years old, cried out for her not to go. She was exhausted and the plea struck her full force.

"I realized then that my sons had no parents," she said. Their dad left and "I was gone all day and all night working." She quit her jobs so she could be with the children and went on welfare. She was able to get a grant to attend school to become a licensed practical nurse.

Working extra shifts helped her barely make ends meet. Then she became ill. She had no health insurance for herself or the boys. "The world was falling apart," she said.

Jensen got little help from the CSE agency. After seven years her ex-husband owed about $12,000 in back payments, she said. She found he was living in another state. She gave his address and place of employment to an enforcement worker. That's when she was told to stop whining and do a better job if she could.

Jensen spends much of her time working for child-support reform at the state and federal levels, helping ACES chapters, being interviewed by the media, and lecturing at colleges and before professional groups.

She is the author of the book, "How To Collect Child Support." An ABC-TV movie, "Abandoned and Deceived," depicted Jensen's life and the creation of ACES.

PART 2
FINDING DEADBEAT DADS

6

SO HE'S FLOWN THE COOP

If he's gone, you'll have to help the CSE agency locate him. You may wind up having to do the job yourself.

That's what this part of the book is about — tracking him down.

Still, you must work with the system's personnel — social workers, prosecutors, investigators, judges, and an array of clerks.

> Many deadbeat fathers refuse to pay because of their anger toward their ex-spouses. It's their way of getting even. But mothers must avoid the trap of letting hostility undermine their efforts to find the absent fathers and get them to pay.
>
> Keep in mind that your goal isn't revenge, but to do what is best for your children. This takes not only determination, but a cool, methodical approach.

Most of the people whose help you need are public employees, either at the county or state level. They are required by law to help locate the absent parent and get him to pay. But like any of us, they have their workloads and their bad days.

It may require an extra effort to get your case moving. It's important to deal with CSE workers in a positive way. Avoid criticizing them without real cause. You want their cooperation, not their anger. Let them know how urgently your children need help. Show them pictures of your children and also of the non-paying dad.

Even when paternity of the dad is established, you may face other hurdles. The father may disappear so he can't be legally served. You can help by furnishing any information about where he may be living or working. The more information you can give enforcement workers the better.

Knowing his Social Security number is essential. It's the best way to confirm a person's identity. It is unique, like fingerprints. With it, you can lock on to the right person if he's listed in driver's license data or other computer files.

If you don't know his Social Security number, you might get it from these other records: voter registration, hospital stays, police reports, income tax returns, court cases, credit cards, insurance policies, and employment files.

ELECTRONIC POSSE

The CSE office can ask the State Parent Locator Service to do an online search of the state's databases of such records as unemployment benefits, workmen's compensation, driver's licenses, motor vehicle registration, income tax, and correctional facilities.

The office can ask another state to search its records, and at the same time ask the Federal Parent Locator Service (FPLS) to try to find the missing dad.

The federal locator can search for a current address in computerized records of the IRS, the Social Security Administration, the departments of Defense and Veteran Affairs, the National Personnel Records Center and reservists and military files. Any information that might be helpful is relayed back to the state or local enforcement agency.

Geraldine Jensen, a leading authority on child support, stresses the importance of using state and federal parent locator services. Government studies, she says, show that 52 percent of absent parents who are found had been located in the same state as their last known address, or at least in an adjacent state.

Some applaud the FPLS system; others argue it too often takes months to respond. The information comes in fragments and is quickly outdated because the person may have moved to a new place or job.

Also, the system doesn't help if the deadbeat's Social Security number isn't known, or if a fake number or a stolen identity is being used. Another criticism is that the state and federal locator services are too limited in their searches.

PHANTOM HEAD COUNTS?

Just how many absent and deadbeat parents are being found through use of state and federal locators? That's difficult to answer. Each year, CSE officials publish state-by-state totals of the number of non-custodial parents supposedly located. But in many instances the numbers are greatly distorted.

In a recent year, 10 states had a location rate of 200 percent or better

— meaning they had computer hits on twice as many people as they were searching for. Another 14 states had better than a 100 percent score. Overall, it appeared the states averaged 92 percent in finding their quarries. How could this be?

Leora Gershenzon, a California attorney active in child support projects, explains that a missing parent can be counted as "located" even if he or she can't be found. The name need only appear on a screen in a computer data match.

And if the name turns up more than once, the location ratio goes up. He need not be found physically. Some call it a phantom count.

FIND HIM YOURSELF

You may be unhappy with the agency's efforts to find your child's father and fear your case will be among the 80 percent in which support goes uncollected.

But don't give up. You can find him on your own. It will take determination, hard work, a search plan, help from others, your own knowledge, memory, imagination, and a little luck. It could be a long-term project.

Think about recruiting a relative or friend to help in the search and reach your goal. Another person could do some of the research and legwork and may have good ideas and contacts. Also important is the support a helper can provide in keeping up your morale . You'll be less likely to quit.

At the start, we suggest you do a quick search of computerized records and data bases to find an address, telephone listing, property holdings, relatives names, or business ties. Maybe you can use the computer at your public library to access databases, or hire someone to do it for you. We deal with this issue in Chapter 11, "A Magic Bullet May Find Him."

If the quick search fails to turn up his name and current address, get organized for a more extended search. Learn what records are available, what they contain and where to find them. You may find clues to his whereabouts that aren't in any database.

You may not be an experienced investigator, but if you organize your thoughts and write in a notebook what you know and what you find, you will have a record of your project.

Keep a special section in your notebook for the names, telephone numbers, and addresses of sources who have helped you, or might be able to. List social workers you talked to, law enforcement contacts and court clerks — almost any employee could become your ally.

THINGS ONLY YOU KNOW

You know things about your quarry that a seasoned detective would love to know: his character, organizations he belongs to, his work, hobbies, skills, education, experience, habits and his preferences, whether it be in foods, sports, sex or climate.

You can arrange your notebook by major categories or sections, perhaps along the lines below.

PHYSICAL CLUES

In one section, jot down his vital statistics — date and place of birth, Social Security number, parents, and his children and their ages. Write down a physical description of him that includes not only his height, weight, color of hair and eyes, but any special markings, such as tattoos or scars from injuries. Does he wear eyeglasses or contact lenses?

Make a note of any surgeries or dental work he had. You might never use this information, but it could become valuable in helping law authorities identify him if he denies who he is.

He can change his name and the color of his hair, but there are some things he can't disguise. Is he right or left-handed? What's his shoe size? Does he wear a dental plate or have something distinctive about his teeth? Does he use a hearing aid or wig?

Get a copy of his most recent driver's license, with his photo. While you're at it, collect other pictures of him and make copies that can be distributed during your search.

HIS PAST, FAMILY AND FRIENDS

Your notes should include towns where he has lived and street addresses, if you know them. If he served in the military, jot down any thing you can remember about his branch of service, dates served, places he was stationed, and his job specialty.

List any property he owned or sold, his investments, what kind of cars he has driven and his driving record.

Few people who disappear can completely cut themselves off from their past. Even when a runaway dad takes a new name, he may drop his guard at times because he doesn't think there's a risk of being found. He may keep ties to relatives — particularly his parents — and an old buddy or girlfriend.

They may tell others about hearing from him.You could learn of his calls and whereabouts by talking to friends and acquaintances you and he once had in common, and any relative who might help you. Ask them to call you if they learn something new. This is one way police find fugitives.

SCHOOL DAYS

Another section of your notebook should focus on his educational background. List the names and locations of all schools he attended, from elementary grades through high school, trade schools or college.

He may stay in touch with the school's alumni office or with old classmates. They may have his latest address, occupation and employer, or information about a past or upcoming reunion. Yearbooks may offer clues about his school activities and old chums.

Some alumni associations, even at the high school level, publish a directory listing all of the school's graduates and their addresses, and possibly phone numbers.

WORK HISTORY

Try to list jobs he has held — where he was employed, the address, and the dates he worked there. If you know, write down the name of his boss or supervisor and any fellow employes you can remember. Chances are the employes may know more about some part of his life than his family does. Often a company where he has applied for work may ask his old employer for a recommendation or to verify that he had once worked there. Ask the former employer if he's heard anything about your deadbeat.

Employers usually keep the original application forms that their employees filled out. These may yield valuable information. When he worked for one or more companies, he may have belonged to a labor union with a local and national base. You might ask local labor officials to check to see if he is still listed as a union member, and if so, where.

Does he have certain skills that he might now use to earn a living? Could he be working as a cook, carpenter, gardener, accountant, salesman or teacher? Could he be in business for himself? Might he advertise in a newspaper for customers?

HABITS DIE HARD

Jot down his habits and preferences. Knowing these traits can pay off. We recall a case in which a prominent woman's husband disappeared and St. Louis police were trying to find him. She told detectives that he liked seafood, sports and writing. He disliked cold weather.

The detectives, using sources, discovered he was in Florida. They were able to find him by checking restaurants, including one he frequented because he liked the seafood there. He had run off and was working under an alias as a sports reporter for a small newspaper.

Suppose the absent father is an ardent fisherman. If he's moved to a new city or state he might have applied for a fishing license, using his own name, rather than an assumed name.

Had he subscribed to a magazine about fishing? Call the magazine and ask that they check the mailing address they used for him. Or you might resort to the non-delivery ploy. You complain that for some reason you haven't been getting the magazine and want to verify where they are sending it. Also, information brokers can search databases that include address changes by magazine subscribers.

People with intimate knowledge of a runaway dad probably know what states or cities that he might have gone to. That could be a big help in targeting him geographically when you begin your search.

ASK YOURSELF THESE QUESTIONS:

• Does he like small town life or the big city? Would he locate near a city with professional sports teams or certain restaurants? Would he head for the beaches, or the mountains?

• Would he likely try to do the same kind of work he had been doing before he disappeared? If not, what other job skills might he rely on?

• Would he stay in contact with old friends or relatives, especially his mother? Might he even continue to donate to his alma mater, attend reunions, or be on the alumni mailing list?

• Is he a military buff who wouldn't miss a chance to attend a reunion of his unit, or a mock Civil War battle, a show involving vintage planes, or a motorcycle rally. If you know he's a fanatic about such events, would it be worth your while to stake out an event to see if he shows up? He might be on the group's mailing list.

• What kind of entertainment does he like? Is he likely to sign up for the symphony, museum or foreign films? Or does he favor rock music, auto racing, or porno flicks? The answers may provide clues on where to begin looking.

This Prosecutor Will Put You In Jail

Leah Haub has enjoyed her work as a prosecutor, even though it means putting about 100 deadbeat parents in jail each year.

Haub

She's headed the child-support division of the prosecutor's office in St. Charles County, Mo., near St. Louis. As an assistant prosecutor, she goes to court nearly every day, establishing paternity, filing motions to modify support awards, getting wage assignments, or handling trials.

She hasn't flinched at urging judges to send deadbeats to jail in misdemeanor and felony non-support cases when they flout the law. "There's a saying around this office that it's always a good day when someone goes to jail," she said.

"When push comes to shove, and I realize I am not going to get any support money from this deadbeat for his children, then I have no problem requesting that he go to jail," she says.

Haub handled Missouri's first felony non-support case. It involved a deadbeat mom who was on the run for four years, living in three other states. When the woman returned to Missouri and took a job, Haub's investigator found her through employment records. She was arrested and paid $8,610 in back support.

About 95 percent of the deadbeats are men, Haub says. "The women deadbeats, I think, are much worse than the men... they don't even try to make excuses for not working and not paying child support," she said.

In one case, she had a father arrested when he returned to his home on a visit after having moved to Alaska. He owed about $12,000 in support. He faced a felony non-support charge, but escaped a jail sentence by paying $3,000 towards what he owed and pledging to make payments on the rest.

Haub got a jail sentence for a 42-year-old deadbeat dad who owed about $15,000 in back support to his son, 6. He hadn't paid *in five years. He lived like a hermit in a rural shack without an indoor toilet. His public defender showed jurors a photo of his portable toilet seat, but it didn't win much sympathy for him.*

Haub told jurors there was no medical evidence that he was unable to work. He said he had quit a job at a pizza place because he didn't like working around "young kids, because they're punks."

"Obviously he's not going to pay this child support no matter what we do to him," Haub said in urging a jail term. "It's time to tell this deadbeat and others like him that we won't tolerate [such] behavior any more."

After nearly ten years in child support laws, Haub remains enthusiastic. "I'm not tired of it. I enjoy it," she said. "There are a lot of people who get frustrated with the whole system. They are rather cynical by the time they hit our office. It's rewarding to show them that the system works after all and for them to get a check."

"I think we have made a difference in these children's lives. I can think of cases where we gave bright young kids a chance to complete college when their deadbeat dads have been forced to cough up $20,000 to $25,000 to stay out of jail," she said.

7

GETTING OTHERS TO HELP

To get people to help you find the father, don't come on like gangbusters. Our advice is to go with a low-key approach. This may involve using psychology on your part.

Whenever we're asked by a stranger to help or do something, we usually make up our minds in a matter of seconds. Salesmen know this. So do investigators, and they tailor their approach to get people's cooperation. You too should be ready to present your case quickly and in a friendly way.

Whether contacting people in person on by phone, figure out your approach beforehand and what their reaction might be. Will they welcome your inquiry, be neutral, or hostile? It's important that you put them at ease.

PUTTING PEOPLE AT EASE

But don't be coy or too subtle. Be matter-of-fact. If you're trying to find a deadbeat dad, let people know of your hardship without whining about it.

You're a good mother and you're doing this for the children. Have a photo of the children handy. It may help convince a social worker or even a stranger to give special attention to your case. Some mothers make their own flier, complete with photos of the children and the deadbeat dad. It's a great attention-getter.

Most people are caring human beings and will help you if you can develop good rapport with them. If their contact with you is unpleasant, they may avoid you or put your case on the back burner.

If you are trying to get information that may get your sources in trouble, assure them that you will not disclose their names or any help they gave you. This is an approach that reporters often use.

HUNTING HIM BY PHONE

The telephone is the easiest and most direct way of locating a deadbeat dad who has moved to another area.

Assume you're about to call someone who might know the father's whereabouts. Mentally rehearse what you will say, even to scripting your questions. Be ready for any question you might be asked, such as why do you want the information, or "How do I know who you are?"

From the outset, establish who you are and try to gain their confidence the same way as if you were face-to-face. You should give them your number so they can call you back and confirm who you are.

Concisely state your reason for calling, what information you are seeking, and why you need it. As you ask questions, you should also be a good listener. Be alert for any off-hand remarks that could help you. If you are given names or phone numbers, write them down.

WHEN ALL ELSE FAILS....GET SNEAKY

Geraldine Jensen, ACES founder and president, suggests various investigative techniques in her book, "How To Collect Child Support II."

"When all else fails, get sneaky!" she writes. "Check the contents of the non-payor's trash. The U.S. Supreme Court has ruled that once trash is put out to the curb, it is public property. Therefore, it not illegal to take the trash and check it out for information about the non-payor such as the names of banks and creditors."

One ploy that Jensen says ACES members have used with a high degree of success is to call non-payors and ask them if they will take a few minutes to answer some survey questions, such as their favorite cars. Later questions might deal with their income bracket, age, type of employment and where employed.

Jensen writes it's not illegal to phone someone and ask survey questions provided you do not mislead the person by saying you are representing a business. If the person volunteers to answer, "it is perfectly legal," she said.

LONG DISTANCE SLEUTHING

If you suspect the father has fled to another state, zero in on the likely city or area when asking an information operator if the deadbeat is listed. Also ask for a street address. The operator may say the person has an unlisted number. Then at least you'll know that he, or someone with the same name, lives in the area.

In cases where there are many listings for a name you're inquiring about, the operator may tell you that you can get three listings at most at any one time. Another problem is that the operator may not have done a wide-area search. And maybe you can't pin down the community you want.

Don't despair. Your local telephone company may have phone books of the cities and their suburbs you're checking. Or they may be at your public library.

Many libraries also have CD-ROMs — compact discs for use with computers — with millions of phone listings covering groups of states or regions. (More on this in Chapter 11).

CHECK THOSE CITY DIRECTORIES

Several companies publish municipal and county directories listing people, their addresses, phone numbers and other information.

They can help you find and contact people who can help you in your search.

When tracking a deadbeat, there are two ways to use these directories. One is to focus on the place where you know he lived for some time. The other is to try to find him listed in a city or state you suspect he has fled to.

Why trace his former residence? By checking directories over a period of years, you may be able to record changes in his addresses, occupation or spouse. And you'll be able to make a list of his former close neighbors, their addresses and phone numbers. One of them might help you locate him.

Suppose you have only a telephone number for your deadbeat, perhaps given to you by a former neighbor or acquaintance of his. You can look up the number in a directory's numerical telephone listing. This will give you a name and address for the number listed — maybe his name or the name of a friend he's staying with. You might get more information about the person listed by cross-checking the name in the alphabetical listings.

The directories can be expensive, but you may be able to access one at the public library, police or sheriff's office, assessor's office, city hall, county courthouse, Chamber of Commerce or the local newspaper. If you need information from a directory in another city, you might ask the library there for help in running down a specific name or address.

Sometimes, peoples' names might not appear in a directory for various reasons. They may have just moved to the area or have been gone several years. They may be using a different name, have an unlisted phone number, or decline to be listed to protect their privacy.

Unlisted telephone numbers sometimes continue to show up in city directories when they no longer are available in the telephone book. That's because some people discontinue their listing in the phone book, but neglect to delete their number in city and cross directories.

HERE ARE SOME OF THE DIRECTORIES AVAILABLE:

R. L. POLK & CO.

Polk, founded in Detroit in 1870, publishes about 1,400 city and suburban directories in the United States and Canada.

The Polk Directory is published periodically and has four major categories: (1) an alphabetical listing of the names of all residents in a given community; (2) an alphabetical listing of business and professional firms; (3) an alphabetical listing of streets, with the names of residents at each address; (4) a numerical sequence listing of telephone numbers, along with residents' names and addresses.

The directories have other valuable information. For example, they usually list a person's street address, city, employer or occupation, telephone number, and the person's marital status, including the spouse's first name and possibly her occupation.

Polk says the information in its directories is based on face-to-face interviews with residents and businesses. They are produced primarily for marketing purposes and are purchased mostly by businesses. Customers include insurance, real estate and financial planning firms and local, state and federal government agencies.

Polk can be reached at 1-800-635-5522.

COLE INFORMATION SERVICES

Cole, based in Lincoln, Neb., publishes more than 150 reference directories. The directories have two sections. One section is an alphabetical list of street names, with the addresses in numerical order. Next to each address is the resident's name and his or her telephone number.

The other section lists phone numbers numerically, and gives the phone subscriber's name and address. Areas served by Cole include the New York City area and communities in such states as Texas, Pennsylvania, Louisiana, Colorado, Washington, Utah, Oregon, Tennessee, Minnesota, Arizona, Kansas and Missouri.

Cole both leases and sells it directories. The firm can be reached at 1-800-438-6093.

HAINES & COMPANY CRISS+CROSS® DIRECTORIES

Haines, of North Canton, Ohio, publishes directories in 69 major markets and suburban areas across the nation. Its Criss+Cross® directory lists residents and businesses — arranged by street and house numbers and by telephone sequence. The address section, for example, lists the name and phone number of anyone living at a specific address. The listing often indicates the number of years the person has been listed at that address.

The company can also provide Criss+Cross directories on CD-ROM and operator-assisted look-ups nationwide, as well as a national on-line look-up with access to 100 million listings from your computer.

Criss+Cross directories are available on an annual lease basis and many libraries across the country have them.

Haines publishes directories for communities in 12 states: Ohio, Georgia, New York, California, Illinois, Indiana, Virginia, Maryland, Louisiana, Kentucky, Missouri, Michigan, and Washington, D.C.

Haines & Company can be reached at 1-800-843-8452.

8

FINDING HIS TRACKS

The more you know about someone, the better your chances of tracking him down. His past may yield the clue that leads to his whereabouts today.

FROM BIRTH TO DEATH WE LEAVE A TRAIL

From the moment we come into this world, we begin generating a trail of records — starting with a birth certificate, and in some cases a public announcement in the newspaper. There may be a baptismal record at a church. Even an infant now gets a Social Security number.

As a child, we do things that add to the paper trail. We attend school, take part in athletics and may join a Scout troop or other youth group.

With each activity the trail lengthens. The records mount until we die. A death certificate then records our passing. But that may not be our last record. There may be an obituary telling others about our life and mentioning our family members. These pieces of information may be helpful in finding a relative or anyone else.

Then there are probate court records that may help in your search. There may be a will, a list of heirs and relatives, and inventories showing the existence of property holdings and other assets we were not aware of. There may be gravestones and cemetery records that yield family information.

When you want to find someone don't think on a grand scale. Instead, think of those everyday things that we all do. Ask yourself what records do those activities produce. Then look for his footprints in the things he does.

WE GO TO SCHOOL. From the first day of classes, we create our own data trail. Our names appear on class rosters. Each year, we meet new teachers and friends who may remember or stay in touch with us.

We get grade reports and diplomas. Our pictures are in the yearbook, sometimes with a brief summary of our activities. School libraries, or faculty members who oversee publishing the yearbooks, are likely to have copies of them, as well as the students.

The school a person attended usually indicates the area where he lived. There we might find former neighbors and friends — some of whom he may still have ties with, or know where he is. From grade school through college, the person may be on an alumni roster or attend class reunions. The organizers of reunions frequently go to great lengths to locate their missing classmates.

WE READ. Besides subscribing to a magazine or newspaper, we may have a library card or book club membership. If your deadbeat is an avid reader and you think he may have moved to a certain community, you might want to stop by the library there and show library employees his photo. If you need to explain why you're looking for him, just show pictures of his children that he's not supporting.

Some people have been known to track down an ex-spouse through his magazine subscription. Their ploy is to call the magazine to ask why copies are not being received. They ask what address the magazine is using. The same approach can be used to see if he is subscribing to newspapers in the towns you suspect he may be living.

WE WORK. This creates a unique history for each of us. Think of the application forms and personnel files that record our starting and leaving of each job, how much we were paid, any promotions, special recognitions or disciplinary actions, and where we moved on to. We leave behind co-workers and bosses who know about us. Our work records will list prior jobs, addresses, telephone numbers, and other data that may point to our whereabouts.

We generate income tax returns that may be examined by a joint filer, such as the spouse or ex-spouse. The tax return may become public in a divorce case or government suit. A job-related injury may produce a workman's compensation or disability claim. If you want to know if a person is working for a company just call that company and say you want to verify employment. Most firms will do so without question so as to help their employees obtain credit, rental housing or other services they have applied for.

When you think about a person's work, consider whether he or she must be licensed or registered by the state. Doctors are. So are other professionals, such as lawyers, engineers, real estate and insurance agents, and securities brokers. Such registrations are usually public records. In the case of an insurance agent, for example, you should be able to find his address, how long he has worked in the field, and what firms or brokers he is, or has been, licensed to represent.

Others who may be regulated by federal, state, county or municipal governments include police officers, nurses, paramedics, barbers, beauticians, undertakers, taxi drivers, watchmen, handlers of hazardous materials, pilots, gun dealers, and other occupations depending on the government jurisdiction.

And don't forget about membership in a union. Millions of the nation's workers are members of some union and their names are on file. They pay dues. They receive mailings from the union. They are known by fellow members.

WE DRIVE. In many states, anyone can check another person's driver's license, driving record and offenses. It's all part of the public record, along with the vehicles owned, including the license plate number, and the vehicle identification number (VIN). Public access to such records is somewhat restricted under a law passed by Congress.

Some states require people buying vehicles to disclose the name of the lender if they got a loan. This bit of information can be useful in finding where an ex-spouse banks and what assets he has. You can request copies of all these driver-related records from state agencies that regulate motor vehicles.

Sometimes we have accidents that lead to lawsuits. The suits would be on file at the county courthouse and may indicate if someone was injured or filed an insurance claim. There may be paperwork relating to injuries in police reports. As a spouse, you may be able to access these records and discover the new address of your former husband.

WE PLAY. If a person swims, golfs, plays tennis, works out, dances, rents videos, or travels — he may join a club. A quick phone call, using a direct question, may verify his membership. In other cases, a more subtle approach may be needed. Some callers have been known to pretend to be the person they are seeking and then ask if his dues are paid up, or if they have his current address.

In many states, boat owners are required to register their boats, just as motor vehicles are registered. You should check the state agency that handles boat licensing. Yachts and larger boats may be registered with the Coast Guard.

WE JOIN GROUPS. You may be able to figure out what groups or organizations your ex might join to fulfill his social needs while in hiding. Was he a member of an American Legion post or other veterans group? If he transferred his membership, someone in the Legion may tell you his new post.

Depending on his line of work, the missing dad may keep up his membership in professional associations and continue to receive their literature. You might call the organizations and ask them to verify his membership and mailing address. The same may be true of other civic, social or religious groups he belonged to.

WE BUY THINGS. In so doing, we leave a trail of receipts, checks, credit card transactions, credit ratings, loan records, liens, and sometimes lawsuits. To protect themselves, many department store chains and other lenders use the Uniform Commercial Code (UCC) to record with the state or county various loans or installment purchases made by consumers or firms.

For a fee, you can obtain a copy of UCC filings that appear under the name of a person or company that bought something on credit. The buyer or borrower might not realize his transaction is part of a public record.

You might find that he put up as security assets you didn't know he had, such as real estate, securities, equipment, accounts receivable or other items of value, including jewelry. The UCC records may be on file at the city or county recorder of deeds, or in a state office, such as the

Secretary of State.

Privacy For Sale

Few details of our finances remain secret, due in part to huge computer networks. Getting a person's credit report is easier than many people think. Jeffrey Rothfeder, investigative reporter and author, described in his book, "Privacy For Sale," how easy it was to get credit reports on former Vice President Dan Quayle, TV anchorman Dan Rather, and then-Congressman Dick Durbin of Illinois. One reviewer applauded Rothfeder's book for exposing the often illegal information underground.

Rothfeder said for under $50 paid to an information company, he was able to access with his home computer many of the private details of Quayle's finances, including his shopping habits and his mortgage. The report showed that Quayle once had shopped frequently at Sears.

One source sold to Rothfeder data on Rather's credit transactions. They showed that Rather was a frugal man given his income and status. Rather had eight credit cards, and on his two major cards, he was paying less than $600 per month in payments. An information source gave Rothfeder TV personality Vanna White's phone number for free. He got her answering machine and left a message. But when he called her two weeks later, her phone number had already been changed.

Other firms are equally anxious to provide such information — at a price, of course. How does one find a data seller? Look in the Yellow Pages under credit services.

Some credit services sell access to personal information in the top part or so-called "header" of a person's credit report. The header information may include the subject's date of birth, Social Security number, current and former addresses and perhaps the spouse's name and his mother's maiden name. Although credit-reporting agencies must comply with certain restrictions because of privacy concerns, they can make the header material available.

The three giant credit bureaus are Trans Union Corp, Experian (formerly TRW) and Equifax. Between them they are reported to have several hundred million credit files in their databases, including more than 160 million individuals. Look them up in the Yellow Pages.

WE PAY BILLS. We heat and cool our homes. We use a telephone. We water the lawn, shower, wash our dishes, and do laundry. We watch TV or do our ironing. All the while, utility companies keep a record of what we owe. In the case of telephone records, they may yield information about a missing dad and who he's called. Perhaps the records include a forwarding address. You may be able to get law enforcement officials or others to access the records or make inquiries for you.

In one instance, the two authors were stymied in locating an engineer they needed to interview for an investigative report. He had worked in St. Louis and moved to a small town in northeast Missouri. But he had moved again and the trail was cold. We called the town's police chief and he took up the challenge to find the man. He put our call on hold, made a call on another phone and came back minutes later with the man's new address in Chicago.

"How did you do that?" we asked. He said he simply called the town's water department's billing clerk at city hall and got the man's forwarding address. Days later, we went to his apartment building in Chicago and rang the doorbell to his second-floor apartment. The engineer came on the intercom, saying "Who's there?" The authors didn't want to risk him refusing to see them.

We answered "hello, hello" to each of his inquiries as to who was there, as if the intercom wasn't working. Finally he came down to see who was there. When he opened the door, we walked in, shook his hand, and began the interview. Out of politeness, he welcomed us in.

Tax payments are public records and may yield information on the person's whereabouts. If your ex owns property find the address where the tax bills for real estate or personal property are being sent.

Federal and state income tax returns are available to each spouse if they filed jointly. There are times when a person's earnings records and tax returns end up as a public record, such as in a divorce case, a civil suit over business dealings, or in a government prosecution for fraud or non-payment of taxes.

WE VOTE. Election officials ask to list our present and former addresses. They record our date of birth, Social Security number, and sometimes our mother's maiden name. In most places, voter registration cards are public records. They tell what elections we voted in, and may include a forwarding address for an absentee voter or a resident who has moved to a new jurisdiction.

WE BREAK THE LAW. It could range from a minor traffic violation to a felony charge. Something as insignificant as a parking ticket can lead to startling disclosures. Police in New York City captured notorious serial killer David Berkowitz, known as "Son of Sam," by linking Berkowitz to a parking ticket issued in Brooklyn on the day he shot and killed his seventh and last victim. His car had been ticketed near the murder scene. Police tediously checked for tickets handed out in the area that day.

You can check at a county courthouse for criminal and civil cases possibly involving your runaway dad. In a civil case, he could have been a defendant or plaintiff. The case files will contain lawyers' names and legal documents, such as subpoenas that lists the person's address.

Lawyers or police officers involved in the court cases might help in tracking down your quarry. They could become valuable allies. Besides county courthouses, it may pay to check records in federal courts, including bankruptcy filings.

WE MARRY. Marriage licenses are usually recorded at the city or county level in the recorder of deeds office or marriage license bureau. They include the application that shows the couple's addresses, the woman's maiden name, the names and addresses of the parents or guardians if one of the applicants is underage, the church or place where the wedding took place, and who officiated at the wedding.

WE DIVORCE. Alas, love and marriage often end in divorce. Was he divorced before or after you and he split? Check the divorce records. They may include addresses, claims and counterclaims, allegations, and questions and responses relating to income, assets, and work history.

The files will also include court rulings on custody, support payments and other issues in the divorce case, along with names of lawyers. There may be orders of protection in the files. You might want to contact any other former spouse for information about him.

WE OWN PROPERTY. From records in county courthouses, we can construct a chronology of all real estate bought by the person we're seeking, or his relatives. The records will tell us from whom he got the property. Often records may show how much he paid, the amounts of any mortgages, and the lender.

Real estate records can be gold mines of other information. They can include facts about someone's finances, and personal and business matters. In the next chapter we'll explore how to look up real estate records and what can be gleaned from them.

A Cop Catches His Deadbeat Mom

Police officer Jim Schweppe spent at least four years chasing down his former wife to make her pay child support for their son.

Schweppe

He had paid child support regularly for four years when she had custody of their son. But when he got custody, she paid for a while and then disappeared.

Schweppe, with the St. Charles, Mo., police department, remarried and had three other children. His ex-wife also remarried and lived in Texas, Nevada and California. She did office work, sometimes for moving and storage companies.

He said when she had custody his ex-wife had moved to Texas with their 9-year-old son and cut off contact. "For almost a year she wouldn't let me see him or even talk to him," he said. Schweppe said he had tried to regain visitation rights, but then sought custody of his son and got it.

Three years later she agreed to pay support of $35 a week. She did, for about 18 months, and then took off. "For four years she gave no support for our son. She wouldn't call and she wouldn't send him birthday cards," Schweppe said.

Schweppe worked with child support agencies in trying to track the deadbeat mom as she moved about ten times through four states. One address checked by authorities turned out to be a jail, he said.

"She was changing jobs and moving from place to place," Schweppe said. "Sometimes it would take a year to find out where she was." He said it would take the CSE office about two months to notify her by letter about paying the support. "A couple of months after she received it, she would be gone to some other area."

State and federal parent locator systems were asked to find her, but with no success. Schweppe said he would prod the CSE agency or have others help him check records every few months. "I tried to stay on top of it. I was just a number in a stack of files."

The break came when Schweppe learned that she had moved back to the St. Louis area and was using her maiden name. Her Missouri ID card, similar to a driver's license, popped up in a computer check by police.

Her address and maiden name turned up in state employment records, showing her as working for an area moving firm. She was arrested in a St. Louis suburb not far from where Schweppe lived.

She became one of the first deadbeats in Missouri to be charged with felony non-support under a new law. She pleaded guilty to a misdemeanor charge and was given two years probation. She paid $8,610 in back support and agreed to pay ongoing support of $35 a week.

After paying the back support, she continued paying weekly support for nearly two years, until her son joined the Navy. Schweppe said the custody and child support fight took an emotional toll on everyone, adding:

"That's the tragedy of the whole deal."

9

HIS PROPERTY MAY RAT ON HIM

With a little help, you can compile from county or city records a list of all real estate owned by your child's father, his relatives or others he had dealings with.

You can trace the history of each property in the county where they were acquired, including transactions that go back decades. Limit your search to dealings in the last five years or so.

In the process, you could find his current address. You'll see the names and addresses of those he dealt with, such as a notary public, and they might help you locate him.

Real estate records are filed at the recorder of deeds office in the county where the property is located. Employees in these offices are usually willing to help search the records. Tell them briefly what you are trying to do.

Look up your own family's property records as a way of familiarizing yourself with how the records are kept and how to search them. Make notes as you go along.

If the recorder's office has computerized records, it can provide printouts of property transactions. Examine the deeds themselves, rather than just the index entries, to avoid errors and get more details about the transactions. Your search may take you into other counties or other states. But you will be on familiar ground because real estate records are quite uniform across the nation.

A WORLD OF GIVERS AND GETTERS

In real estate, the world is made up of two groups that we'll call Givers and Getters. The more formal labels are Grantors and Grantees. All property records are set up in these two groupings, even in century-old land records.

The givers — or grantors — are people, firms or institutions that convey property to another party. They may give it away, sell it, trade it, or bequeath it. The givers are listed alphabetically in the Grantor book, sometimes called the Direct Index. Under each grantor's name is a listing of his or her transactions.

The Grantee book lists the names of people or firms who receive property or certain rights, such as an easement or right-of-way. These books may be called the Indirect Index, the Reverse Index, or the Inverted Index.

The grantor and grantee books are kept by the year. They list the dates of the transfers, a brief description of the property, and the pages in the deed books, or on microfilm rolls, where the documents can be found.

Always check entries in both sets of books. A man buying a home can wind up in both the grantor and grantee books. If he takes out a mortgage, he becomes a grantor by pledging to repay the loan.

RECORDS ARE REVEALING

The books may cite liens filed by the government or private parties, grants of oil and gas exploration rights, and easements. There may be notations about marriages, divorces, deaths, wills, and other probate matters.

The makeup and status of limited partnerships, changes of names, and other tidbits find their way into real estate records.

Each time you find your deadbeat dad buying or selling property, and a company is involved, check the deeds or other documents for names of officers who signed for the company. Could he have a financial interest in the company? Check the Secretary of State's office to see who the officers are.

Sometimes an owner conceals his interest in the property by putting it under the name of a "straw party" — perhaps a friend, a secretary, janitor or other employee. To avoid any foulup on payment of taxes, the true owner may have the tax bills sent to his own address, but still using the straw party's name. That address — available at the tax collector's office — may help identify the actual owner.

QUESTIONS TO ASK

- Who is likely to know your quarry's whereabouts or his place of employment? Are there banks, lenders, businesses or individuals who would know?
- Should you approach these sources straight on? They might be cooperative. But they might refuse to give out the information, or even worse, notify your deadbeat dad that you had inquired about him. You might not want to tip him off that you're on his trail.
- You may want to have someone else make the inquiry, such as a friend who has been helping you, or a child support enforcement worker.

Belinda McGrath: How She Did It

When Belinda McGrath read an article in the Detroit News with the headline, "Looking For Mr. Deadbeat," a light went on in her mind. She clipped the article, thinking it could somehow lead her to paydirt. What follows is her account:

Because her ex-husband did not pay the child support her two daughters needed, McGrath had to go on welfare for about a year. "I lived out of suitcases and boxes," she said.

She had married her high school beau. The union was troubled and they divorced. She said he gave her only sporadic support payments, then none at all, and also stopped seeing the children.

Five years later and 30 years old, she was living in a mobile home in Sterling Heights, Mich. She had no idea where her ex-husband was. At that time, she said, "I just wanted him to leave me alone." She got training at a business college and worked several years doing accounts payable for a small firm. Her mother watched the kids.

Detroit Free Press

Belinda McGrath with daughters Megan (left) and Andrea.

Eventually, McGrath decided it was unfair for her children not to get the support they needed. "I decided I would go after him for child support," she said.

When they divorced, McGrath had gotten a court order that called for him to pay only $45 a month for his two daughters. She knew he worked as a contractor and heard that "he was doing quite well." But how could she find him, and make him pay?

The newspaper article, by David Farrell, appeared about this time. It offered both inspiration and a guide. It gave tips on how to track a person down using driving records and other public information. Following another tip, she said, "I made a list of people he hung out with and what skills he had."

Following the article's advice, she checked county records and found he was licensed to build and sell homes. She found that his vehicles were licensed to his company. With high hopes, she turned the information over to the county child support collection agency, called Friend of the Court.

"I was told I had to get his actual address," she said. His business license listed his parents and she had only a post office box for his address. From old chums she learned that he was operating a successful business.

"I did the things listed in the article. I was determined to find him," McGrath said. From high school friends they both knew, she learned he drove a big red truck and had recently bought a house to rehab. She went to the county recorder of deeds and checked through computer records.

"One day I was sitting at a computer and his mortgage popped up. I was so excited. I had an address and papers showing he owned a house."

"One day I was sitting at a computer and his mortgage popped up. I was so excited. I had an address and papers showing he owned a house."

She learned from a realtor that her ex-husband had planned to fix up the house and sell it. She struck out trying to get information from the bank he used. "I would pretend I was his wife," she said.

With the new information she supplied about his finances, the Friend of the Court agency got an order raising the child support award to $187 a month. He didn't show up for a court hearing, and "I won by default."

But won what? She still wasn't getting the money. She would drive by the house he was rehabbing, sometimes peering into a Dumpster to see old fixtures and debris, and noticing new windows he installed. "His money is going into this house. I was good and mad. The kids and I needed the money," she said. He was $7,000 in arrears and "to me and the girls that was a lot of money."

He finally moved into the house, but she couldn't get police to do anything. "I wanted him arrested, but they said it was the business of the court....they said not paying child support was not a serious *crime." She finally got a bench warrant issued for his arrest, but the court deputies weren't very interested in finding him.*

"I was pretty upset. I called the local newspaper. I was going to do whatever I had to do," she said. She got a reporter at the Detroit Free Press to include her in a story about child support. It told how her ex-husband had missed eight court dates in a row. The article included a picture of McGrath and her two daughters sitting on the front porch of their mobile home.

Court officials were embarrassed and soon an officer called, wanting to know where he could arrest her ex-husband. "I told him where he stopped for breakfast each day and that he'd probably be sitting outside near a pay phone making business calls.'" (She had learned this from friends). She had his truck license number and old pictures of him. The officer found him at the pay phone just as McGrath had said.

He was arrested, but got out of jail within an hour after posting a $1,600 bond. "The judge turned that over to me and the kids," she said.

He said he didn't have any money, McGrath said, but his family started making some payments and soon he became more regular with the checks. "It was due to my being persistent," she said. "After he was arrested it opened his eyes."

"The girls and I can now do a little better," McGrath said. Her oldest daughter got to go to a Girl Scout summer camp, "something we couldn't otherwise afford."

McGrath worked her way up to a sales job for a large telephone company, sold the mobile home and moved into a house. "My children have suffered by not having a father," she says. The oldest wonders why her dad won't see her. One Christmas, the youngest girl said all she wanted was a dad.

McGrath attended meetings of ACES and started helping other women who weren't getting their child support. She talks to groups, especially teen moms about how they can get off welfare. "I like helping others find people and get information about assets," she said.

10

CLONE HIM

You may be able to find your deadbeat by cloning him from records, various bits of information, and even gossip.

CREATING HIS PROFILE

By cloning, we mean to recreate on paper a life-like profile or model of someone, in this case your deadbeat dad.

No matter how well you think you know him, you may be unaware of clues that could be helpful in finding him.

By going through the cloning process you can uncover many details about his past and perhaps what he's been doing since you split. You can do this even when he's in hiding or refuses to cooperate with you or the authorities.

A SECRET HIDEAWAY?

Don't be afraid to ask people about him. You may find that he owns property that he's never told you about. There may be a friend or new lover he shares a cabin hideaway with.

Try to gather everything you can about his physical appearance, marital and financial status, property holdings, work, education, updated background, his friends and acquaintances.

To get or verify his date of birth and Social Security number, one place to look is voter registration records.

County or city registrars often record our date of birth, Social Security number, and sometimes our mother's maiden name, along with our addresses over the years. The voter registration cards are public records in most places.

Other sources for getting a date of birth and Social Security number are driver's licenses, divorce records, and lawsuits — civil or criminal — that he may have been a party to.

DRIVER'S RECORDS ARE GREAT

Driver's license records have always been one of the first places to look. Each state has up-to-date records on everyone who drives. Besides a person's photo, address, height and weight, they include such descriptive data as color of eyes and hair.

In many states, a driver's ID number is the same as his Social Security number. Driving offenses, accidents, and disciplinary actions are also included. The number and kinds of vehicles that a driver owns is usually listed.

These records have always been public in most states. However, because of privacy concerns and federal legislation, some states have restricted access to the records.

Check with the motor vehicle registry in each state where you suspect he may be. They will tell you if the records are public and how to access them. (See next chapter for more on these records).

County circuit court files may tell you a lot. Check his name for both criminal and civil cases, such as a divorce from another woman. In a divorce, both the husband and wife are asked to provide a sworn accounting of their sources of income, their assets and indebtedness.

If the split is unfriendly, or the amount of money in dispute is great, opposing lawyers are apt to focus on personal details during deposition-taking and courtroom testimony.

Besides local courts, you may want to see if the deadbeat has been involved in federal bankruptcy court, or been in a criminal or civil case in federal court.

As you finish cloning your deadbeat dad — your notebook should be full of details from the records you reviewed, the names of people you contacted and the results. What seems unimportant today may turn out to be significant later.

PLACES TO LOOK

Police, private detectives, and investigative reporters often use lists that tell them what kind of records and documents they ought to be looking at and what people to talk to. Lists help us organize our thoughts and search efforts.

If you draw up a list of records to check, try to arrange them in some order of priority. At the top should be those records your intuition tells you have the best chance of producing leads for finding the person.

HERE ARE RECORDS OR SOURCES WORTH CHECKING:

- Driver's licenses, car registrations, and driving records
- Marriages, divorces, births and deaths
- Property deeds, mortgages, options
- Telephone and other utility bills
- Phone books and information operators
- Criss+Cross and other directories
- Union membership
- Employment and job application records
- Assessments and property tax records
- Credit reports and jointly held charge cards
- Moving companies, hauling rentals and storage facilities
- New utility services, cutoffs, forwarding addresses
- Postal changes of address
- Hunting and fishing licenses, gun permits
- Lawsuits, both civil and criminal, and police records
- Pet licenses
- State, federal tax returns (when jointly filed)
- Newspaper, magazine, cable TV subscriptions
- Theatre, symphony and museum memberships
- Club memberships: video, book, health, and auto club
- Cancelled or microfilm copies of checks from joint accounts
- Military and government service records
- Wills, power of attorney, probate inventories
- Payrolls, budgets, expense vouchers, receipts
- Voter registration rolls
- Election and campaign finance records
- Planning and zoning applications, permits and hearings
- Business licenses and permits
- Professional registrations, licenses and directories
- Church, social, professional, and other group memberships
- Hobby or sports interests
- Uniform Commercial Code filings

- Firms' incorporation papers and reports filed with state
- Securities and Exchange Commission
- Workman's compensation and disability claims
- City auto stickers, parking permits
- Accident claims and insurance records
- Trash pickup and billing records
- School records, yearbooks, alumni and reunion groups
- School district mailings
- Neighborhood associations
- Adult education classes
- Tax and property liens, mechanics liens
- Library cards
- Favorite charitable donations
- Newspaper reference files, or microfilm copies at library
- Building, zoning permits
- Bankruptcy court filings
- Residential inspections, occupancy permits
- State government manuals listing employees.

11

A MAGIC BULLET MAY FIND HIM

TRY A QUICK, LONG-SHOT DATABASE SEARCH

When using a database for your search, as cited in earlier chapters, you may want to try, as a long shot, using a "magic bullet" — a marvelous new technique in problem solving.

The right "bullet" might be one of three categories of files as the most likely source of your much-sought information. They are: 1) Motor Vehicle and Driver's Records, 2) CD-ROMs and Computer Databases, and 3) Records of Organizations

A GOOD FIRST CHOICE: DRIVER'S RECORDS

Each state keeps records of people with driver's licenses and the vehicles they own.

These have long been open to the public, although some restrictions limiting access to them have been imposed in recent years.

Your deadbeat dad's license record has a wealth of information that might help you locate him. Besides his name, it lists his date of birth, possibly his Social Security number, address, his height, weight, and the color of eyes and hair. If he's required to wear eyeglasses while driving that may be noted, along with any other restrictions.

The state's records will show whether a person has been cited for drunk driving, speeding, or other traffic violations. They may pinpoint where the violations occurred, providing a possible clue to the driver's whereabouts. The records list the type and number of cars or trucks owned by a person or business, the model and year, the VIN (vehicle identification number), and often where, and from whom the vehicles were purchased.

MURDER OF ACTRESS TIGHTENS ACCESS

Because of privacy and safety concerns, federal legislation has forced states to tighten access to these records. It was prompted by the murder of 21-year-old television actress Rebecca Schaeffer. She was shot at her Los Angeles home by an obsessive fan. The killer had paid $200 to get her address from a private detective, who got it from her driver's license record.

The states must allow motorists to "opt out" when applying for a driving license or renewing a license. That means they can tell the states not to release their names and other personal data.

But traffic violations and accidents remain public record even for those who opted not to have other personal information disclosed.

There are some agencies and people who can continue to get the information about those motorists who opted out. Among those allowed access are government agencies, courts, police, insurance firms, tow truck operators, car dealers, employers of commercial drivers, mass marketers, researchers, in some states news reporters, and — ironically— private investigators. Maybe you can get help from someone with access to the records.

Some states have gone further than others in denying public access to the motor vehicle records. In states where a driver's record is closed, you may be able to get some of the same personal information from voter registration records.

OLD DRIVER'S RECORDS STILL ONLINE

And don't forget that millions of driver records, dating back about a decade, are still in the computerized files of database firms which routinely had obtained them from the states before the restrictions.

Driver information is usually kept by the Secretary of State's office or the state's Motor Vehicle Registry, often a division of the state's Revenue Department. It helps if you know the person's full name, date of birth, Social Security number and the town or city he may be staying in. This will help differentiate the person you are seeking from others with similar names or initials.

You may have to spread your net to more than one state, going through the process in each of them. There is no nation-wide database for motor vehicles and drivers, but some firms have databases that include many states.

If you score a hit and find the name, date of birth, or Social Security number that matches your quarry, you can then check to see if he's still at the new address listed. You or someone else could try to secretly spot him or his vehicle at the location.

USING CD-ROMS AND COMPUTERIZED DATABASES

No matter how private we try to be, billions of pieces of personal information — about where we live and what we do — find their way into computerized files and CD-ROMs that can be electronically retrieved in minutes. The files include nation-wide listings, often broken down into regions, of persons whose names appear in telephone or street directories or other databases.

HERE ARE SOME SOURCES FOR THE INFORMATION:

Consumer credit reports. Changes of address. Magazine and direct mail lists. Births, deaths, marriages and divorces. Voter registration. Education history. Employment, benefit, and personnel records. Workers compensation claims. Driver's licenses. Vehicle, boat and plane ownership registration.

Military records and locators. Property holdings, past and present. Relatives and neighbors. Corporation records, fictitious name registration. Uniform Commercial Code filings. Bankruptcies. Liens, lawsuits, civil and criminal judgments. National death index and other Social Security records. Hospital and medical records. City and county directories. And hundreds of other records.

You can access these records in two ways: do it yourself, or hire someone else to do it. Some database firms will search their records for you.

DOING YOUR OWN SEARCH

There are CD-ROMs — special compact discs — that contain millions of telephone subscribers by name, address and telephone number. You can buy these discs for use on computers that have CD-ROM players. Your public library may have them available for free use. If your local newspaper has telephone discs, maybe it will let you use them.

CD-ROM stands for Compact Disc Read-Only Memory. They are

similar to the music CDs that are used in home stereo systems. But computer CDs can store vast amounts of data, graphics, and video segments.

You can make a state-by-state search for the person you are seeking. It's as though you suddenly had before you copies of telephone directories from hundreds of cities. But you can get buried under a mountain of similar names in the various cities. Many of the listings may use just initials with the last name.

That's one argument for trying to focus on those places where he most likely would be. Use the most current telephone discs available.

You may be lucky and come up with a quick match. But there are often gaps and mistakes. Many names that should be listed simply aren't. Names that are in telephone directories sometimes can't be found in computerized databases. This is not surprising, given the enormous task of combining new and old listings.

Another problem is that your deadbeat may have an unlisted number or is using a different, or slightly different name. Some telephone discs may be outdated because area codes have changed.

You can also go to your library or local telephone company office to see if they have current phone books for the cities you want to check. That way, you can more easily explore the pages and make copies of them. You can check the names you find against a municipal directory, such as the Polk Directory, that lists residents, their addresses, occupations, and spouses.

Some libraries may have listings of phone books from various states and larger cities on microfiche. University Microfilms International provides a nation-wide Phonefiche of 2,500 phone directories covering 50,000 communities.

CD-ROMs that include both residential and business listings are being marketed by several firms and the competition has brought prices down. A U.S. Supreme Court ruling held that telephone companies can not copyright their directories and this has allowed data firms to use the listings on CD-ROMs. Ask about them at your library or at office supply and computer stores. One firm said it had virtually every listed phone number and home address in the United States, along with street maps.

DATABASE SERVICES THAT CAN HELP

The gathering and selling of personal data has become big business. For a fee, some firms will let you tap into their files. In some cases they themselves may be tapping into databases compiled by other companies.

There are more than 10,000 databases and hundreds of on-line services that provide access to many of the databases. You can check your Yellow Pages for people-finding services.

GALE DIRECTORY OF DATABASES

A better bet would be to see if your library or newspaper has a copy of the Gale Directory of Databases. It's published periodically by Gale Research (1-800-877-GALE) in two volumes. One recent edition of the directory identifies about 10,480 databases. It describes some databases that can be used in finding people and the on-line services to access them.

Atlanta-based Information America has compiled from public records a number of databases that are useful in finding people, as well as some of their assets. It's owned by West Publishing of Eagan, Minn., which also owns WESTLAW®, an on-line provider of legal information.

Information America's databases are generally not available to the public, but can be accessed by law firms, major corporations and governmental agencies that subscribe to WESTLAW. The cost can be expensive.

Information America has databases on millions of individuals and households. The information includes family name, current address, telephone number, date of birth, length of residence, family members and up to ten neighbors with addresses and telephone numbers. Other databases include property liens and judgments, corporate and limited partnership records and asset locators.

Information America can be reached at:

One Georgia Center
600 West Peachtree St., NW
Atlanta, GA 30308
1-800-235-4008

A rival firm, LEXIS-NEXIS, based in Dayton, Ohio, also has compiled people-finding databases, and a mountain of legal issue files.

LEXIS-NEXIS can be reached at:

9443 Springboro Pike
P.O. Box 993
Dayton, OH 45401-0933
1-800-227-4908

COMPUTERIZED SEARCHES

Some database firms will do the search for you for a fee, giving the results by phone, letter or fax. Others allow you to access their files. Check the cost beforehand as the fees can be high. Some firms charge a set amount while others bill for the time involved.

Some companies may limit access to their records to law officers, insurance representatives, lawyers, private investigators, prospective employers, creditors, or reporters. They want to avoid any complaints of improper use of the data. If a firm won't let you search its records for a deadbeat dad, try to recruit someone eligible to do it.

THEY'LL DO YOUR SEARCH FOR A PRICE

Here are some companies that do name searches:

FIND PEOPLE FAST — A Service of Infomax, Inc,
Post Office Box 20190, St. Louis, MO 63123
1-800-829-1807 Fax 314-631-5785

This search firm is run by Graham Bloy and Dan Buescher. Some lawyers use the service to locate people, such as deadbeat dads. The firm says it has more than 170 million adults listed in its databases.

For a search, it helps to have the first and last name of the deadbeat. But the more information the better. The customer gets a list of names, addresses and phone numbers matched to the name provided. It's up to the customer to check out the names to see if they include the person being sought. Anyone can use the service.

Within minutes, the firm's computer can make searches nationwide or focus on a region, state or city. Expanded searches can involve checking Social Security numbers, changes of address, driver's license records, death index, motor vehicle records and credit bureau records.

The data are compiled from a number of sources, primarily voter registration records, direct mail lists, phone directory information and other public records. Most customers are women, between ages 25 and 55, seeking family members.

The firm has gotten widespread publicity. It can't guarantee finding people who don't want to be found because they may have been able to keep their names out of the databases. But Bloy says it is getting harder to hide: Anyone who subscribes to a magazine or buys something may have his name put on a list sold to a marketer. "You can hide for six months or so, but sooner or later you will show up," Bloy said.

THE NATIONWIDE LOCATOR

Post Office Box 17118
Spartanburg, SC 29301
1-800-937-2133; FAX (864) 595-0813

Lt. Col. Richard S. Johnson (Ret), an expert in finding military personnel and other people, founded Nationwide Locator after a 28-year career in the U.S. Army. His agency first focused on locating people in the Armed Forces, and then expanded its scope. Johnson said it can provide addresses and other information from huge databases to people seeking friends and relatives, and to attorneys, private investigators, collection agencies and reunion planners.

Its services are open to anyone. In most cases, responses are mailed or faxed with 24 hours of receipt of the request for help, Johnson says.

With just a Social Security number, Nationwide Locator says it can usually identify the person, his or her most current reported address, and prior reported addresses, if the number is contained in a national credit file. The agency can also do computer searches using a name, date of birth and other information, such as a telephone number.

Johnson says staff members have had success using just a first name and date of birth. This is important in cases where a man or woman may have taken a new last name.

WORLDWIDE TRACERS

P.O. Box 173006
Arlington, TX 76003-3006
(817) 473-0449 or 1-800-432-3463; FAX: (817) 473-0113

"If I take a case for you, I never close it until we solve it," says Pat Rutherford, owner of Worldwide Tracers. He says the company handles many child support cases and has gone to Germany, France and elsewhere in Europe searching for deadbeat dads.

"Computers have completely changed our methods of locating people and have made these searches affordable and practical," Rutherford said. "With the data banks available today, no one can hide." The firm also can do what it calls a continuous search, with updates each six months, in cases involving missing fathers.

YOU CAN LINK UP TO DATABASES

There are firms which, for a fee, may allow you, your lawyer or a friendly police officer to access their files by using a personal computer and a software package or code provided by the firms. They include:

DBT DATABASE TECHNOLOGIES, INC.

100 East Sample Road, Suite 310
Pompano Beach, FL 33064
1-800-279-7710; (954) 781-5221
FAX: (954) 781-2756

DBT is an online search firm that allows you to access its databases using your own computer. If you've got a name, or just a Social Security number, it can usually kick out a report crammed with details on the person. It may include personal data such as date of birth, past and present addresses, telephone numbers, neighbors, relatives, vehicles, assets and other information culled from public and other records.

The firm says that a client, with a single keystroke, can search the entire nation for a person. There's one catch: they won't give access to everyone, for fear some may abuse the information. Law enforcement officials, lawyers, insurance firms, investigators and reporters are among those allowed.

The fee is based on the online usage time. Clients are given a computer disc that allows them to access the system 24 hours a day. They need to set up a user ID and a password. The firm will help clients and says computer experience is not required.

To access the files, you'll need an IBM-compatible computer with a modem. Printing out the data would reduce online time.

In a demonstration for one of the authors, using only his name (with middle initial), the online service pulled up his and his wife's Social Security numbers, state of issue, and their children's names. It found his date of birth, telephone listings, past and present residences, relatives and neighbors' addresses and phone numbers, drivers license data (including height, weight and color of eyes), and vehicles owned and their estimated value.

The search and printout took about five minutes.

US DATALINK, INC.
6711 Bayway Drive
Baytown, TX 77520
1-800-527-7930

This database firm does pre-employment background screenings to protect company assets against embezzlement, fraud or theft, as well as corporate intelligence.

It also does people locator searches and skip tracing. It can provide information about where someone works, or has worked. Its clients include major companies, banks, hospitals, utilities, universities, newspapers and private investigators. One client is a child-support collection firm.

ALERTS — FROM MAIL DROPS TO FAKE NAMES

US Datalink taps into a large network of records and research reports. It said it has quick access to records across the country. One result is that it can provide employers with reports that alert them to mail drop addresses, fraudulent Social Security numbers, and the possible use of assumed names.

The firm says it can do nationwide checks of records such as criminal conviction histories, driver's license reports, Workers Compensation claims, education histories, prior employment, professional licensing and Social Security numbers verification.

US Datalink provides computerized access for a set fee. Or, the client can access information sending FAX forms. Specific types of searches carry varying fees. It says its records aren't on-line as such. Instead, the firms said it offers research reports compiled by a network of 1,400 professionals.

RECORDS OF ORGANIZATIONS

There are governmental agencies, as well as public and private organizations that can help you locate the person you are seeking. Often, they can provide an address that may not be available elsewhere. Or they might direct you to another source that you haven't thought about.

For example, the Salvation Army operates a Missing Persons Program that helps reunite thousands of families each year. And mothers can track down deadbeat dads who are in the military through the military's locator system for the branch of service the dad is in. Unions keep rosters of their members. You may be able to locate a runaway dad by checking the Postal Service's change of address records.

Access to some of these files may be restricted. Here's a rundown of agencies that could prove useful:

SALVATION ARMY'S MISSING PERSONS PROGRAM

The program is an international service that helps reunite family members who have lost contact and wish to find each other. Because of privacy concerns, the agency will not divulge an individual's whereabouts without his or her consent.

Except in unusual circumstances, the program does not take on searches involving legal matters, inheritance or estates, adoption cases, persons missing less than six months, and genealogical requests. A Salvation Army spokeswoman said that, in general, cases involving child support are not accepted. Exceptions might be made, for example, if a child is dying or the father's medical history is needed to diagnose and treat the child's illness, the spokeswoman said.

Searches may involve government offices, credit and social service agencies, and law enforcement personnel. The agency evaluates requests on an individual basis and may accept or deny an application. Salvation Army officials are concerned they might get flooded with requests that they cannot accept.

To request a search, you must contact the Missing Persons bureau in the region where you live, rather than the last known locale of the missing person.

Here are the telephone numbers for the Salvation Army's four missing persons bureaus:

Central Territory, Des Plaines, IL (847) 294-2000
Eastern Territory, West Nyack, NY 1-800-315-7699
Western Territory, Torrance, CA 1-800-698-7728
Southern Territory, Atlanta, GA 1-800-939-2769

MILITARY LOCATORS

Mothers may be able to track down deadbeat dads by using the military locator system for the branch of service the dad is in. The computerized system can be used to help find active duty and reserve personnel. Reasonable search fees are charged. See chapter 13 on locating veterans and other military personnel.

SOCIAL SECURITY ADMINISTRATION

Each year about 25,000 people ask Social Security for help in locating a missing person. Although the agency's records are kept private, it says it may forward a letter to a person, "if there's a compelling humanitarian or financial reason and it is reasonable to assume that the missing person would want to be notified." If the person sought is receiving Social Security benefits, the agency may mail the letter directly. If the person is not receiving benefits, the letter is sent in care of the last employer on the person's Social Security earnings record. After a letter is forwarded, it is up to the missing person to respond, or not. Social Security takes no further action.

Give the name and Social Security number of the person you're looking for. If you don't know the number, include his place and date of birth and his parents' names. You may want to include a copy of your driver's license to prove your identity to the agency.

In the case of a missing dad, you would write a separate letter to him and place the letter in an unsealed stamped envelope that has his name and Social Security number on it. Place these in a second envelope and mail it to:

Social Security Administration
Letter Forwarding Service
Office of Central Records Operations
300 N. Greene Street
Baltimore, MD 21201

One spokesman all but rules out the likelihood that Social Security will forward such mail in deadbeat dad cases. But, he says Social Security does help child enforcement officials by allowing them access to its records. Ask your caseworker to make such a request.

INTERNAL REVENUE SERVICE

The IRS will forward a letter to a person if you can convince the agency that you have a humanitarian reason to justify sending such a letter. You should provide the person's full name and Social Security number. If you don't know the number, provide his date of birth.

Send your request letter to the IRS in an envelope that also includes the stamped letter you want sent to the missing relative or person. Your letter should emphasize strongly the reason(s) for your request, which might focus on his family or children's health and welfare.

Call 1-800-829-1040 to reach an IRS representative who will provide you with the address of the IRS office where you should send your request. If the IRS agrees to forward the letter, it would go to the dad's last known address in the IRS files. The IRS is prohibited from disclosing his address.

U.S. POSTAL SERVICE

In recent years the Postal Service, because of privacy concerns, changed its policy of allowing people to go into a post office and get the new address of a person who had been in the office's service area. Though you can no longer do this, the new address may be available through a database firm. Here's how:

The Postal Service maintains a National Change of Address system (NCOA), which includes millions of address changes. This helps mailing list companies update their addresses. The changes can be purchased by brokers who then sell them to direct marketers, various database firms and also private investigators, skip tracers and others. You should ask them whether they can get the change of address for you, and how much would they charge.

If it's practical, talk to the letter carrier who last left mail at the missing person's last known address. The carrier may remember where he moved to, or help you find his new address. Post office rules prohibit carriers from disclosing changes of address, so you may strike out. But maybe his one-time neighbors might know where he moved to.

Here's another approach that might work: Send a test letter to the missing person's old address, but mark on the envelope: "Return Service Requested." Make sure your return address is on the envelope. If the letter can't be delivered as addressed, it is returned to the sender with the new address. If the post office does not have a forwarding address it will indicate on the envelope the reason for non-delivery.

AND THEN THERE'S THE INTERNET

Using the Internet is still a practice of a minority of people in the United States. But it can give you access to information from thousands of sources. It can let you tap into information stored in federal, state and local computers. It can help you find addresses for millions of people. It can even draw maps for you.

We'll explain next how you can use the Internet to locate someone. It depends on whether his name shows up on any of thousands of websites that you can visit via computer.

Diane Smith: Got Her Interstate Case Rolling

Imagine getting bawled out by caseworkers because you're trying to get child support for your son.

Smith

It happened to Diane Smith of California when she tried to get her caseworkers in Alameda County to cooperate with Illinois authorities on her interstate case.

Her son's father was living in Chicago and had been paying support through a wage assignment. This stopped in 1995 when he left his job as an airline flight attendant.

"Cook County (Ill.) found out he was working again. Alameda County didn't know he was working," Smith said. "I spoke with Illinois and they called Alameda County.

"This got some people in the Alameda office very upset. They bawled me out."

She said they told her they got a call from ACES and threatened in a letter that if she had anything to do with the self-help group the agency would drop her case.

"I couldn't believe it. It was ridiculous. This case was about a child, not who has the power," Smith said.

She gave this account of her case:

Her son was born in 1980. The father then moved to Chicago. Smith had regularly been receiving $425 a month in child support. The dad stayed in touch with his son, and would make visits to California and take him places.

Smith had worked as a skin care specialist and later for a telephone company. She was injured in a fall and suffers from chronic pain. She was unable to work, and then the absent dad was out of work.

Child support payments stopped and Smith wasn't sure what to do. Visits to her son also stopped. "I thought he'd get back on his feet," she said. Nothing happened for a year and a half and she decided she had to start pushing her case. Her son needed remedial help for a learning disability. Diagnosis and tutoring were costly.

"I drafted a letter and put down everything I knew about him, his job, 401K plan, last home address and other information," she said.

"He was always a working person. I'm the one who lagged on pursuing it," Smith said.

She contacted ACES and eventually got help from Geraldine Jensen, the group's founder, who contacted someone in Cook County, Smith said. "A woman from the state agency called me and said she would contact Alameda County."

She Was 'Stepping Out Of Line'

It was then that the Alameda caseworkers got upset. "I was told I was stepping out of line," Smith said. "Their reaction to ACES was negative."

She admits to being persistent, but says it was in the interest of her son. She said she was supplying information that child support authorities in California should have obtained in the first place.

At one point, a deputy district attorney for Alameda County told her that they had served Cook County and were waiting for a court date to be set. "I said, 'Why? I have a wage assignment order and federal law says this order should be honored.' "

"I didn't have to wait for a court date. My child support was already established. I had to remind them of that. I was waiting almost a year," she said.

Smith had done her homework on the URESA and USIFA laws governing interstate child support cases.

She urged the prosecutors to go to the father's employer to withhold the child support. They did and Smith started receiving it again, albeit with a three-year lapse that resulted in an arrearage of about $10,000, she said.

After support payments were again being made, her son and his father resumed their relationship. "Interstate collection takes a long time," Smith says. "The more information you can give to the DA, it will expedite collection. You have to call and do much of the work on your own."

Smith is now taking college classes and is a chapter leader for ACES. When she was interviewed by the authors she said she was helping a California woman who was trying to get $108,000 in back child support from an absent father who was in Massachusetts. Smith said the man had transferred property to another person and said he had no income.

12

TRACKING HIM ON THE INTERNET

Virtually every federal agency and thousands of state and local agencies are on the Internet. So are universities, organizations, businesses and a ton of databases. If you have access to a computer and can get online, you might pull up the name or even the whereabouts of your deadbeat.

HERE ARE SOME THINGS YOU MIGHT BE ABLE TO DO ON THE NET:

• Find him through "people finders," which use records such as phone listings.

• Find him if he's licensed through his occupation, or perhaps as a hunter or pilot.

• Find his name on an alumni list, and maybe his address too.

• Find his name in public employee listings.

• Find his e-mail address, if he has one, and it may lead you to his home address.

A MOUSE CAN COVER A LOT OF GROUND

With a few clicks here and there, you can call up whole telephone directories, as many as 80 million residential listings, millions of e-mail addresses, street addresses and neighborhood maps, listings of government employees, prison inmates in some states and licensed occupations.

Some states have made it easier for citizens to see listings of persons in jobs licensed by the state. The listings, already in agency computers, are easily put on the Internet. Here are occupations that may be listed:

Barbers, cosmetologists, manicurists, pharmacists, doctors, dentists, nurses, paramedics, emergency medical technicians, podiatrists, psychologists, chiropractors, audiologists, sellers of hearing aids, speech pathologists, teachers, day care operators, athletic trainers, veterinarians, nursing home administrators, clinical social workers, therapists, embalmers and funeral directors.

Also, lawyers, architects, landscape architects, engineers, land surveyors, real estate agents and brokers, appraisers, police officers, CPAs, auditors, insurance brokers, private employment agencies, vehicle inspectors, plumbers and holders of liquor licenses.

Some states are moving to publish online names of many state employees, their occupations, addresses and salaries. The listings may include staff members at state universities, hospitals, mental health facilities, prisons and motor vehicle offices.

You can also be able to find listings of people who hold federal licenses, such as pilots.

"NAKED IN CYBERSPACE"

Carole A. Lane's book, *Naked In Cyberspace: How to Find Personal Information Online,* (Pemberton Press, 1997), is the most comprehensive book we've found in using online resources to get data about people. She writes:

"In a few hours, sitting at my computer, beginning with no more than your name and address, I can find out what you do for a living, the names and ages of your spouse and children, what kind of car you drive, the value of your house and how much you pay in taxes on it. "From what I learn, I can make a good guess at your income. I can uncover that forgotten drug bust in college. In fact, if you are well known, I can do all this without knowing your address. And, of course, if you become a skilled data searcher, familiar with the online resources available to us all, you will be able to learn much the same things about me, or almost anyone else who attracts your curiosity.

"...There is not a lot of real privacy left, and what remains is disappearing fast," Lane notes.

WHAT THE INTERNET IS

The Internet was born in the 1960s by government and military leaders. They wanted to hook up their computers in more reliable ways to be sure of continued communication in the event of emergencies — if, for example, a nuclear bomb destroyed a central computer. For the scientists, a bigger goal was to have a more efficient way of distributing research information.

What they ended up with was a system of computers hooked up in multiple ways. This kind of network allows for fast exchange of information among different sources and recipients — kind of like a computer version of the postal service. The explosion of home computers has made the Internet our society's latest technological wonder.

HOW TO GET ONLINE

The easiest way to get online is to buy a computer, plug your phone line into it, and call an Internet service provider. That is also the expensive way. If you don't have Internet access at home or at work, you may get free access through a computer at a public library.

In some urban areas, you can even find coffee houses that have computers with Internet connections. Connecting through a coffeehouse might cost a few bucks, but at least you can eat a Danish at the keyboard. Those places often are referred to as cybercafes.

Don't let lack of experience on the Internet stop you. Librarians will be glad to help. Cashiers or customers at the coffeehouse might help if you ask politely. You might also find classes on the Internet at a local community college. The college will let you use the computers in class, and train you in how to do it. Classes that meet once or twice a week might cost you about $50.

SEARCHING A MAZE

The Internet is a big mess. Anyone with the right kind of computer can publish on the Internet. And since no one has to check in with someone else first, there's a mass of unindexed information out there. There's no guarantee any of it is accurate. The data is scattered among thousands of Web sites or pages published by public and private groups, and even individuals. Each has its own electronic address. (The terms "Web" and "WWW" come from the World Wide Web, which is essentially a special way of publishing information on the Internet.) The problem is how to search through this maze.

To get online, you need a "browser" — a computer program that allows you to read what's on the Internet. You also need an address to start searching with (we'll give you those in a moment.) You'll enter that address into the browser. Just look for a white box titled "Netsite" or "URL" or "Address" or "Site" or "Go to" and enter the address there.

USE THESE TOOLS TO SEARCH:

People finders are probably your best shot at finding someone. They use license data, phone book data, name searches, assessment records, e-mail addresses, and other records to make name searches, and to gather information about people and businesses.

Search engines, operated by businesses that make money from ads, set up a central computer that stores an index of what's on the Internet. The index is updated daily so you can check the index for Internet pages that mention the key words you have supplied. It'll find a bunch of pages quickly and will rank them by how often and how close together the key terms appear. Maybe the person you're looking for is mentioned on a hobby page or a government page or a corporate page. The search engine will probe millions of pages to look for "hits" — matches — for you.

Directories are more sophisticated than search engines because the pages are not only indexed by computers, but also by humans. Directories identify the best sites in many different categories and subcategories. They can you get to a specific page faster, but they usually contain many fewer sites than search engines.

THREE PEOPLE FINDERS:

InfoSpace (www.infospace.com): Enter a name or part of a name and InfoSpace will give you e-mail addresses, phone listings, street addresses, even maps showing the address of the people listed. It'll also show you information about the towns where they live.

InfoSpace has added a marvelous reverse lookup. Enter a phone number and it may give you the name and address of the person with that number.

WhoWhere (www.whowhere.com): Has U.S. government numbers and addresses, 80 million U.S. residential listings and 10 million e-mail addresses. Names of married women don't always show up in listings.

Bigfoot (www.bigfoot.com): Has 5.5 million e-mail addresses, plus lots of street addresses. A nice feature of this people finder is that it'll show you a map of the street address of the person you've found.

Other people finders are listed elsewhere in this chapter. If you don't find the person you are looking for at one of them, move to another.

DEADBEAT — THE ALUM

Let's say your deadbeat bragged about graduating from the University of Chicago.

Who might have current information about him as a former student? A state agency? Probably not. A bank that might carry the student loan? Yes, but the bank would be reluctant to reveal that information. How about the university. Yes! And what division of the university would work hardest to keep up-to-date records? The alumni office, which hopes he'll respond to donation requests.

With that in mind, let's find the University of Chicago alumni office online. We'll use the Yahoo directory, which is a good place to start when you know of a specific site you're looking for. So we tell the browser to go to www.yahoo.com.

On the front page of Yahoo, we see a list of categories, one of which is Education. We click it, and then we see a list of other categories, including Higher Education. We see yet another list. Click on Colleges and Universities. This takes us to a list of countries. Click on United States. Finally we see a list of letters. Click on U. Now scroll down and look for University of Chicago. Click. Now click on "Alumni Organizations."

On this page, Alumni Gateway is a likely choice, so we take it. And we're there. We click around a little, then find that the Alumni Association has posted a list of e-mail addresses of alumni, sorted by year. If we find our quarry, we can use his e-mail address as a search word in a people finder. This would more likely than not give us more information, perhaps even a home address.

By using their e-mail addresses, you might send inquiries to other graduates in your ex-spouse's field of study and class, asking them if they know his whereabouts.

DEADBEAT — THE FAN

In this example, our quarry is a fan of the late author William S. Burroughs.

The place where really fanatic fans hang out is on newsgroups — computerized bulletin boards. People post messages there, then respond to other people's messages, and so on. They often leave behind names and e-mail addresses or both.

The best way to search the postings on them is to use DejaNews as a search tool. We'll visit DejaNews and do a search on William S. Burroughs. We find a lot of postings in a newsgroup called alt.books.beat-generation. Let's visit it to see if someone who sounds like our quarry has left any messages.

We enter this: *news:alt.books.beatgeneration* in our browser's URL, or address, box. We see a list of postings, and many of them include names and e-mail addresses.

We browse through the messages. If we're really lucky, we'll see that our quarry has signed his name and has left an e-mail address. Use it as a people finder search word.

DEADBEAT — THE HOBBYIST

Suppose your deadbeat is a fanatic about a hobby, such as raising chinchillas. The special search engine DejaNews (www.dejanews.com) searches Internet newsgroups — bulletin boards devoted to particular topics.

You can search on the name of chinchillas and get a list of postings that people entered on the bulletin boards using that word. (One of the bulletin boards, in fact, alt.chinchillas, is devoted entirely to the subject.) You'll also usually find the e-mail address of those who left messages, hopefully including your deadbeat. Again, you can then use that e-mail address as a search word in a people finder.

You can even post a message yourself looking for help, but remember that you'll be revealing something about yourself to the entire world.

DEADBEAT — THE VETERINARIAN

If your runaway dad is a veterinarian, try to get a list of veterinarians in the state or states you suspect he has fled to.

Where would you look? Let's think. The Humane Society might be interested in publishing something like that, but it has plenty of other work to do. And its listings might not be up to date. What about a veterinarian's association? That's a possibility. But it may have lists only of members, not of all vets.

Who does the licensing anyway? A state agency does, and it may publish its list on its own web pages on the Internet. So let's check.

Let's use the directory Yahoo to find the Missouri government page. We'll click on Government, then on U.S. States, then on Missouri, then on Missouri State Government Web. We see a lot of agencies listed there. One of them is the Department of Economic Development, a title that often includes licensings. On that agency's page we see a link to Division of Professional Registration.

We click on that, then we see Directories Online. We click on that, and we see dozens of directories of licensed professionals online including the names of licensed veterinarians in the state. You may have to download the list and browse through it with a database program, but it's likely that many states will soon have those listings immediately available without special software.

A FEW WARNINGS

Just as government and agency listings can be out of date, listings on the Internet are only as good as the most recent update. New sites can pop up daily and old ones disappear.

The Internet itself is always changing. In a few years, Internet information will be available not only on computers, but on TV sets and phone lines. The Internet tends to make printed material stale pretty quickly. Although databases available on the Internet can be useful, they usually aren't as good as commercial databases that are more carefully researched and produced.

Search engines and directories are far from comprehensive. The person you're looking for might be mentioned dozens of times on the Internet, but search engines might be able to find only one mention, or none. It helps if the person you're looking for has added to a listing or intentionally published something on the Internet. This is, of course, not the behavior of someone who's trying to hide out. That means that this kind of search is probably less likely to succeed than an intensive search of public records. The good news: it's less time-consuming.

Another potential goldmine are the archives of newspapers online. Many of them go back a decade or so, and searching those archives can help you dig up references to all kinds of people.

The Internet may not have one single bit of information about your quarry. But if it does, searching it is so fast and cheap that you'd be doing yourself a disservice if you didn't check it out early on. You may find nothing more than a lead, but it might be the right lead.

OTHER SEARCH ENGINES

Altavista (www.altavista.digital.com): Altavista is our favorite. It's fairly fast and comprehensive. As with other search engines, it'll rank hits by relevance, that is, by the relative number of times your search terms appear and how close together.

Webcrawler (www.webcrawler.com): Webcrawler lets you do a search on similar pages, that is, pages that contain the same kind of content as an earlier "hit". That helps to narrow your search a bit.

Excite (www.excite.com): This one is interesting because of its "concept search" function. You can do a search on, say, Camaro. It will pull up pages that mention Camaro, and also pages that mention the words Chevy and Chevrolet. That's because its computerized mind has noticed that those latter words often appear in conjunction with the word Camaro.

DIRECTORIES

Yahoo(www.yahoo.com): This is the king of the Internet directories. Its categories are logical and easy to get around in. If you're looking for a particular agency's or company's page, this is the place to start.

Magellan (www.mckinley.com): This is the cousin of the Excite search engine. You can find nicely done summaries of the sites it searches, but it's not as comprehensive as we'd like.

MORE PEOPLE FINDERS

Switchboard (www.switchboard.com): This fast people finder helps you find businesses, too. It'll return phone numbers and postal addresses. It will let you narrow your search by searching within certain organizations.

Four 11 (www.four11.com): Although the interface — the screen that you work in — is not the easiest, it works well. Make sure you're searching the right directory.

OTHER USEFUL SITES

Ancestry Home Town (www.ancestry.com): This is probably more generally useful for genealogists, but you might find it useful, too. Search the Social Security Death Index (SSDI) to see if the subject of your search is dead.

Newspaper Association of America (www.naa.org): The hot links section of this page lists hundreds of newspapers that have online publications. You might be able to find online archives at some of them.

Phonebook Gateway (www.uiuc.edu/cgi-bin/ph/lookup): You can search through phone books for hundreds of colleges here.

Child Support Newsgroup (www.news:alt.child-support): This is a newsgroup, not a Web site, devoted to the topic of child support. If you can't get help here, you might be able to at least commiserate with others.

Justice Information Center(www.ncjrs.org): This page, a service of the National Criminal Justice Reference Service, carries a list of criminal justice-related sites on the Net.

13

IF HE'S IN THE MILITARY

Army regulations require soldiers to provide financial support for their families and obey court orders on child custody. The Navy, Air Force and Marines have similar regulations.

If your deadbeat dad is in the military, ask your child support enforcement agency to get his address and current assignment by using the appropriate military locator for the branch of service he's in.

This also can be done for a person who has retired from the service or has been discharged. The request should be made in writing on the CSE agency's letterhead.

Give your enforcement worker any relevant information you have about him, including his full name, date of birth, Social Security number, service serial number, hometown, rank, job assignment, when he entered the military and his last known unit or address.

Unhappily, the record of some states in locating absent parents in the military has been a poor one.

A federal study several years ago based on a survey of military cases in eight states showed the states weren't collecting support payments in more than half the cases surveyed. If court orders were enforced, the study said, the government could save $54 million in welfare and Medicaid costs as most of the families were on welfare.

YOU CAN USE THE MILITARY LOCATORS

Mothers, on their own, can also track down deadbeat dads by using the military locator system. The computerized locators can turn up both active duty and reserve personnel.

A $3.50 fee usually is charged by the service branch locators for each name you submit, but some requests are free.

Each service branch will tell you the unit to which he is currently assigned, unless he is stationed outside the U.S. You can ask them to forward a letter to him. Place it in a sealed stamped envelope and put it in a larger envelope addressed to the service locator with your request to have it forwarded. Include a fact sheet telling as much as you know about him in the service.

The Air Force Locator, for example, will forward a letter to members of the Air Force Reserve and Air National Guard. It will also provide the unit of assignment, except for overseas units on active duty.

To locate someone who is or has been in the military, here's a list on where to check, courtesy of retired Army Lt. Col. Richard S. Johnson, a nationally recognized expert in the field.

Air Force Active Duty, Retired and Reserve, and Air National Guard:
U.S. Air Force World-Wide Locator
AFPC-MSIMDL
550 C. Street West, Suite 50
Randolph Air Force Base, TX 78150-4752

Army Active Duty:
World-Wide Locator
U.S. Army Enlisted Records and Evaluation Center
8899 East 56th Street
Indianapolis, IN 46249-5301

Army Reserve:
Army Reserve Personnel Center
ATTN: DARP-VSE
9700 Page Blvd.
St. Louis, MO 63132-5100

Coast Guard Active Duty:
Commandant
(CGPC-ADM-3)
U.S. Coast Guard
2100 Second Street, S.W.
Washington, DC 20593-0001

Coast Guard Retired:
Commanding Officer (RAS)
U.S. Coast Guard Pay and Personnel Center
444 S.E. Quincy Street
Topeka, KS 66683-3591

Coast Guard Reserve:
Commandant
U.S. Coast Guard
2100 Second Street, S.W.
Washington, DC 20593-0001
Marine Corps Active Duty and Selected Reserve:
U.S. Marine Corps-CMC
(MMSB-10)
2008 Elliot Road, Room 201
Quantico, VA 22134-5030
Marine Corps Retired:
CMC (MMSR-6)
HQ Marine Corps
2 Navy Annex
Washington, DC 20380-1775
Marine Corps Individual Ready Reserve, Fleet Marine Corps, Reserve or Inactive Reserve:
Marine Corps Reserve Support Center
10950 El Monte
Overland Park, KS 66211-1408
Navy Active Duty:
Bureau of Naval Personnel
PERS-324
2 Navy Annex
Washington, DC 20370-3240
Navy Retired, Individual Ready Reserve and Inactive Reserve:
Commanding Officer
Naval Reserve Personnel Center
4400 Dauphine Street
New Orleans, LA 70149-7800

DEPARTMENT OF VETERANS AFFAIRS

The Department of Veterans Affairs (formerly the Veterans Administration) will forward a letter from you to any veteran on file as having applied for VA benefits. Again, provide as much identifying information as possible, such as full name, birth date, Social Security or military serial number, and last address. Before sending a self-addressed stamped envelope for forwarding, call the VA at 1-800-827-1000. You will be connected to the closest VA office.

Each state operates its own Army National Guard. Contact the state Adjutant General's Office, usually in the state capital, for records of active duty and inactive personnel. You can get the AG's address from any Guard unit or the telephone number from the information operator.

A CLASSIC GUIDE FOR FINDING ANYONE IN THE MILITARY

If you are trying to locate someone in the military, get a copy of the latest edition of a book by retired Army Lt. Col. Richard S. Johnson. He's the author of *How to Locate Anyone Who Is Or Has Been In The Military — Armed Forces Locator Guide.* It's published by:

MIE Publishing
PO Box 17118
Spartanburg, SC 29301
1-800-937-2133

His book lists a myriad of methods for locating current or former military personnel. Johnson and his daughter, Debra Johnson Knox, operate their own people-finding services, based in Spartanburg.

WHERE THE RECORDS ARE

Other records provide clues to the whereabouts of millions of veterans.

The single largest depository of military records is the National Personnel Records Center, at 9700 Page Boulevard, in suburban St. Louis. It has files on more than 50 million discharged or deceased veterans. These include personnel and medical records, some dating to the late 1800s. Most are from World War I or later.

You can ask the NPRC for personnel data, but the request must be in writing, with your signature. Requests should cite the Freedom of Information Act as the basis of the request. The request should be made on a copy of Standard Form 180, but a simple letter might do if it contains the correct name, service or Social Security number, approximate dates served, branch of service if known, your address to send the reply, along with your telephone number.

The U.S. Army Reserve Personnel Center, which shares the same campus as the NPRC, has custody of about 2.5 million reserve personnel files. In trying to locate a reservist, the key is having his Social Security number. A spokesperson told us:

"We can give (the) awards and decorations, assignments, date of birth, marital status, dependents, duty status, where and when, the home of record, but not the exact address. If they are deceased, we can tell you where they died and were buried. We do not release any disciplinary information unless they have been convicted by court martial....A reservist, if assigned to a unit, we would tell you the identity of the unit and the telephone number and address."

HIS DISCHARGE MAY BE ON FILE LOCALLY

Finding out details about someone's military service could be as easy as looking up a copy of his or her discharge from the Army, Navy, Air Force, Marines or other branch of service. Go to the Recorder of Deeds office in the county or city you think that person returned to on discharge and ask for help in looking up the document.

He may have been discharged in the same community that he entered the service.

The copy of the discharge could have a wealth of details: when and where the person was born, race, in some cases; level of education; marital status, date inducted and date and type of discharge; height, weight and other physical data; Social Security number and Selective Service number; blood type; military specialty, such as clerk typist, Reserve obligations, decorations and medals, home of record when inducted, permanent address for mailing purposes, and the person's signature.

14

GETTING EXPERT HELP

AT TIMES YOU MAY NEED A PRO

Take any help you can get to find a runaway dad who is not supporting his children.

Suppose you can't find him on your own, or with volunteer help. Should you pay someone — a gumshoe — to locate him? You'll have to make that decision. When seeking just one person, it may be cheaper to hire someone to make a data search rather than paying the costs involved in going online yourself.

WHO TO HIRE?

You want a person experienced at finding people, such as a private detective or investigator. They are often ex-cops or others who have worked in law enforcement, former child support caseworkers, skip tracers, computer whizzes, or even auto repo men. But there are some flakes in the business who are incompetent or not to be trusted.

Lawyers hire private investigators routinely. Do you know a lawyer, police officer, or anyone else who can recommend a good investigator? Ask around. Get several names, if you can, and call them. Explain what you need.

Ask for references, whether they are licensed and insured, how much they would charge, and what they would provide for a set price. Don't agree to an hourly rate if the case is difficult and could result in big fees.

"You can't imagine how many people have thrown away thousands of dollars on what should have been an hour-long search," says Richard S. Johnson, a highly regarded people finder.

Private detectives are licensed in most states. You may be able to get information about them that they provided in applying for a license. Some states, like Illinois, require that applicants must have an investigative background before being eligible to take the exam.

Illinois requires $1 million insurance coverage on each private investigator and the same amount for private detective agencies. Any person can call the Illinois Department of Professional Regulations and find out whether an investigator is licensed or has been disciplined by the state. Details are not released. It's best dealing with a licensed PI.

Lacking a personal referral, you can try the Yellow Pages to find an investigator. There's also the National Association of Investigative Specialists, based in Austin, Tex. (512) 420-9292. They have about 2,000 members nationwide and can supply names of investigators in your area.

Or try the National Association of Legal Investigators, Inc. (1-800-266-6254). This group was founded in 1967 by 35 investigators and now has about 700 members in 50 states. The association publishes a quarterly journal, "The Legal Investigator."

Anthony M. Golec, a founding member and past president, from Belleville, Ill., said the investigators work for lawyers mainly but also accept cases from the public. The association will provide a person with the names of investigators in the person's area. Golec said the investigators "are all computer literate."

Detectives tell us that a person usually makes the decision on who to hire after talking to the private investigator and getting a feeling about him. Of course, price has a lot to do with it.

WHAT WILL THE PRIVATE EYE DO FOR YOU?

Make it clear to the investigator what you want him find out. Tell him you want him to physically locate your children's father, rather than finding the deadbeat's name and address in some computer database that may be out of date. Tell the detective all you know about the runaway dad.

You should ask the PI to find where the dad works, his income, where he lives, with whom, whether he owns or rents, and his lifestyle. Other questions: What does he drive and what's his license number.

What name(s) is he using? Where does he hang out? Where and when might he be legally served or arrested? You may have to pay more for surveillance work and taking of photos or videos. Many private detectives serve legal papers for their clients.

Investigators check with their quarry's relatives, former friends, and disgruntled girlfriends. They know how to lean on people and pry information from them. This is something you may not feel comfortable doing yourself.

Former cops usually have the advantage of gaining access to non-public police files through friends still on the force. Investigators also check court records, credit reports and databases.

Tell your investigator to guard against letting the runaway know you have located him, so as not to spook him into fleeing again. A word of caution: For your own protection, be sure to ask any investigator or researcher whether he or she uses any illegal means. You could run into problems if the investigator gets hauled into court.

When the runaway dad is found, turn over the information to your child-support caseworker, or your attorney, if you have one.

SWITCH TO COMPUTERS

A New York Times article by Nina Bernstein told how computers have changed the private eye business:

"Private investigators have always followed the footsteps of people's personal lives. But in the past five years the growing power of computers and the expansion of commercial databases have made it quicker, cheaper and easier than ever for private eyes to collect individualized information that their gumshoe predecessors could not piece together even through weeks of dogged surveillance and research.

"...Once mainly the province of retired police officers in tiny offices, the investigations industry is now a booming global business swept by mergers and acquisitions, with revenue projected to reach $4.6 billion by the year 2000, or nearly quintuple 1980 levels. Practitioners range from large, blue-chip business-investigation firms.... to upstart web sites that offer anybody's secrets at bargain rates.

"They all benefit from huge loopholes in the nation's patchwork privacy laws that make the lines between legal and illicit data hard to discern — or easy to ignore — by the time a piece of information has passed through several hands," the Times article said.

A Determined Mom Turns Bounty Hunter

Charlene Dunbar, of Columbus, Ohio, doesn't mind being called a bounty hunter.

Dunbar

That's what she does for a living — chasing down deadbeat parents across the country. She's often featured in stories by the print and broadcast media.

She says she got into the child-support collection business because she knows the plight of mothers and children who are abandoned and often left impoverished. "I've been there myself," says Dunbar.

Her ex-husband quit paying child support for their daughter and two sons. Relentlessly, she tracked him from Ohio to California, Florida, back to Ohio and finally to Texas, she said. At one point her local CSE agency told her it was going to close her case, even though she had an active support order.

Through her own research of the child support laws, and her efforts to force interstate collection, she got her ex-husband arrested. He finally paid about $40,000 in back support.

"It took me eight years," the feisty Dunbar says. "Now I chase other men and women." She took the name Dunbar when she remarried.

She started Children's Support Services of Ohio, based in Columbus, a private collection agency that tracks down deadbeat parents for a basic fee of $175 and then 30 percent of the back support collected. She's aggressive, one day bringing 13 parents into court to file criminal non-support charges against their ex-spouses. The parents said they were fed up with lack of action by the CSE agency and prosecutor's office.

Dunbar had a comfortable life before her divorce. Her husband was earning close to $100,000 a year producing videos, she said, and was to pay $750 a month under the divorce decree. "He paid for a couple of years, then moved out of state. He cut us off."

She said at times she was working three jobs and struggling to sur-

vive. "We were having to sit in candlelight, eating with the electric, gas or water off," she said. "There was a feeling of abandonment. He did what he wanted and that was that." She refused to apply for welfare benefits. "It was never an option as long as I had two arms and two legs."

She gives this account of her long struggle to get her ex-spouse to pay:

Through his work, she tracked him to California. She went to a library and read up on URESA (Uniform Reciprocal Enforcement Support Act), that is used to collect support in interstate cases. Her CSE caseworker didn't know anything about it, so she handled the paperwork herself, getting an attorney friend to notarize it. After a hearing in California, her ex-spouse made three payments totaling $1,050.

He moved to Florida, back to Ohio, and then to Dallas where he was self-employed. She wrote letters to people he contracted with, complaining that he was a deadbeat dad. He contended that Dunbar and her new husband should support the three children.

At about that time, she was told her case would be dropped by her CSE agency because collection was improbable. She went to the prosecutor's office in Columbus and said she wanted to file a criminal charge. "You've done your homework," assistant prosecutor Scott Longo said.

A detective in Texas took pictures of her ex-husband's house and cars in Dallas. He was arrested on a warrant from Ohio and jailed briefly. He pleaded guilty to a reduced misdemeanor charge and then came up with most of the nearly $40,000 she contended he owed, Longo said. He paid the rest in installments. He was put on probation and began making the regular monthly payments.

As for the jailing, Dunbar said: "I'm sorry it came to that. But it was all because he wouldn't pay. He always had the money."

Dunbar says her children grew up not knowing their father. Her daughter was 12 when he left. "She was daddy's little girl. I could see her wanting to be accepted and loved," Dunbar said. Their daughter is married now with children of her own. She took them to Texas for a visit to get to know their grandfather. One son moved to Dallas to work with his father.

Dunbar has this advice for moms trying to get their child support: "You have to be persistent with the county agency. It takes tenacity. It's an endurance test. Don't give up. That's what the ex-spouse wants you to do. Keep knocking on the door."

PART 3

MAKING HIM PAY

15

YOU HAVE AN IMPORTANT ROLE

HELPING THE SYSTEM COLLECT

Finding the delinquent parent is one thing. Making him or her pay is another.

Unfortunately, the collection system is often ineffective and plagued by a backlog of cases. Overworked clerks, social workers and prosecutors may let your case languish. You may have to jump start it. We have talked to mothers who are very frustrated, even bitter, about how their cases seemed to be ignored. Some take out their anger on the caseworkers and become verbally abusive. The caseworkers see them as gripers and tune them out. They respond in kind, which means the caseworkers may bury the files of the complainers. A few caseworkers have been known to throw out a woman's file in retaliation. And some workers even take the side of the deadbeat dad, sympathizing with a man who had such a nasty wife. The workers would rather help the women who treat them well and seem deserving.

Avoid getting into clashes with the enforcement agency and staff members. You need them, and they need your help to get the job done. We mentioned earlier the value of using photos of your children to bring home the human element to caseworkers and others you are asking for help. When someone helps you, a "Thank You" can go a long way. It's best to come across as a reasonable and informed mother who is determined to get the money your children need. Educate yourself on what the enforcement agency is required to do to help custodial parents collect their support. One example: The agency must seek immediate wage withholding through the dad's employer whenever possible. Congress has mandated such wage withholding be included in all court orders. And states are supposed to honor wage withholding orders from other states. Employers are required to cooperate.

As noted earlier, keep a record of all the information you gather about the absent father, especially about his finances. Focus on identifying where he works and how much he earns. This information is vital to caseworkers, prosecutors or court personnel who may seek to garnishee his wages or attach tax refunds to satisfy a support order. Information you give your caseworker should include:

• Name, current address and Social Security number of the absent parent.

• Names and addresses of his current or former employers, or if he's self-employed.

• Data on his income and assets, including any pay slips you have, as well as tax returns, bank accounts, investments or property holdings.

• Information about your own income and assets.

• His current marital status and dependents.

• Your child support order, divorce decree or separation agreement.

YOU MAY HAVE TO RAISE HELL!

Once the deadbeat dad is found, and it's shown he has the ability to pay, there should be no excuse for the enforcement agency failing to collect the child support owed you. Let them know you're angry and upset. At the same time, don't go to war with them. They are your allies and you can't win without them. Be firm but conciliatory, much as someone making a consumer complaint. But the stakes are much higher here. Keep a record of the agency's actions in your case. If you aren't satisfied with your caseworker see if they will assign a different one. Or, write to higher officials and document your complaints. It's harder to ignore someone who puts her plight in writing. One unhappy mother in Michigan carried her campaign — in letters and telephone calls — to the county director of child support enforcement. She got her case moving.

A mother can have her own attorney work to collect support payments through wage withholding. Or the attorney can work through the Child Support Enforcement program to coordinate collection efforts. The next chapter deals with what you, your attorney, or the enforcement agency can lawfully do to make the deadbeat pay. These include the use of wage withholding, garnishments, intercepting tax refunds, liens and other actions.

She Went To Top Boss, Got Case Going

Once Carol LeDuc figured out how to be a squeaky wheel she was able to get the Michigan child support system to find her son's father and make him pay.

LeDuc

Things got moving after she decided to go above the heads of some uncooperative enforcement workers and appeal directly to the agency's top bosses. Mention of the name ACES in her letters and telephone calls helped a lot. LeDuc said she went to a chapter seminar of ACES (Association For Children For Enforcement of Support) and "I learned to contact the appropriate people, the people who count." Before we tell how LeDuc's story ended, here's how it all began:

While dating a co-worker at her job in Detroit she got pregnant. She was 27 and when the baby came he admitted paternity. She got a child support order for him to pay $45 a week, but he made sporadic payments and then stopped.

LeDuc was struggling financially. "I don't know how I did it, trying to raise a child with very little money," she said. But she never went on welfare. The county's agency to collect child support, called Friend of the Court, "didn't do anything to run him down," she said.

But LeDuc decided to pursue him for the money. "I couldn't find him. He fell $7,500 behind in payments," she said.

She attended an ACES seminar in Livonia, Mich. "I found out what the Friend of the Court should be doing and what I should be saying to them. They can access a lot of databases but they don't utilize them like they should," she said.

LeDuc wrote to the director of Friend of the Court in Wayne County, telling him that her son's father was avoiding payments. "You've done nothing to track him down," she said. She requested that he be called in for a show-cause hearing to explain why he wasn't paying. She told the director that her child's father was giving the wrong address for his employer. The director had one of his people contact the firm's main office in another state to get the correct address so a wage assignment could be made. She said she frequently spoke to the director by phone. "I became an ACES chapter leader. The pull I had was the ACES name. It lets them know we're a lot more knowledgeable," LeDuc said. "I got my first child support check about four months after I joined ACES."

Since then, LeDuc said, she has helped other mothers get their child support. A problem some of them had was in dealing with personnel at the enforcement agency. "Friend of the Court was telling people to get their own lawyers. I tell mothers not to do that. Don't spend money on a lawyer. They are supposed to help you."

She said some agency personnel use bullying tactics to get mothers off the telephone or out of the office. "They'll only work the easy cases to get the federal incentive funds," she said. One worker would scream at the mothers and tell them to get a lawyer. Such workers view the women as whiners and some even take the side of the deadbeat dads, thinking they are being treated badly, LeDuc said. "I tell our members not to holler or be belligerent, but act in a calm and firm manner. Some mothers get frustrated. They think I'm going to do it for them. When they find out they have to do it for themselves, they give up.

"If members feel they are getting the run-around and checks are not coming in, I advise them to write a letter, following the chain of command, and to send copies to the state director. Wait a couple of weeks and send a second letter, asking what he will do. Mention ACES or my name."

LeDuc got her support payments raised to $55 a week and began getting checks regularly. She hopes her son's father continues paying support, but adds: "He knows I'm smarter now."

16

UNCOVERING HIS ASSETS

FINDING EVEN HIS SECRET OWNERSHIP

If you want to make him pay, you must find out what assets he has. You're part of a team effort.

But you may have to be the quarterback because you are most familiar with your own case and have more at stake than others who are supposed to be helping you.

Ask yourself:

Does he own jewelry, stocks or certificates of deposit? Does he own a home, condo or land that a lien could be placed against? Does he have a checking or bank savings account that could be attached?

Turn over anything you find to the child support investigator handling your case.

There are firms that can do database searches which could uncover some of his assets. Depending on the state, these records may be available: property and tax assessment records, tax liens, corporate and limited partnerships, bankruptcies, motor vehicle records, Uniform Commercial Code (UCC) filings and state and federal civil law suits and judgments.

MAYBE THE IRS CAN HELP

Under certain conditions, the IRS, working through state and federal CSE agencies, can disclose information from the tax return. This could be helpful in setting the support order amount. It could also help in finding a deadbeat dad and determining his financial assets. This could lead to intercepting his federal tax refund to satisfy past-due support. The information can only be used for the purpose of enforcing child support payments.

For convenience, we have grouped assets into six categories. We suggest ways to identify assets your runaway dad may own — either in his own name, a relative's name or a straw party. The categories are:

- Land and Property
- Bank Accounts, Investments and Securities
- Cars, Boats And Planes
- Jewelry, Furnishings, Other Personal Property
- Ownership in Businesses
- Income and Earnings

LAND AND PROPERTY

As noted in Chapter 9, real estate records may help you find his address or those of relatives where he might stay. The records, usually at the county courthouse, would list any property assets and perhaps those he may have hidden under the names of family members. The records may include entries that reveal probate and inheritance matters, mineral rights, other marriages or divorces, if he lawfully changed his name, and limited partnerships. There may be liabilities too, such as federal, state or commercial liens on property you didn't know he had. The files might include a foreclosure for failure to pay mortgages or taxes.

There may be a *lis pendens* filed — a formal notice that tells potential buyers about pending lawsuits or liens that may be placed on the property. The *lis pendens* could lead you to court cases, where the files may include interrogatories or depositions that shed light on his income or assets.

In some areas, the price paid for a home or other real estate must be filed with the county assessor. This may be done by a certificate or declaration that becomes part of the public record. Many states do not have such a requirement. Even so, you can get from the assessor the value placed on the home for tax purposes.

Knowing what property an ex-spouse or absentee father owns in the county can be important. You may be able to uncover real estate you didn't know about or hidden income, like rent from a property that he quietly owns.

BANK ACCOUNTS, INVESTMENTS AND SECURITIES

If the non-paying father has substantial savings, securities or other investments, the court should know about it. That could be the key to getting him to pay up on what he owes his children. Here are some things you can do:

• Try to remember what assets he ever mentioned or received mail about, like stocks, savings bonds or accounts, and certificates of deposit.

• Are there any pension or retirement funds that his ex-wife has a vested interest in and that could benefit the family upon divorce or his death? List these assets and give them to your caseworker, enforcement officials, or your lawyer.

• Did he get any inheritance, either before or after you were together? If so, did his parents leave an estate that went through probate? Probate court records identify the heirs and include an inventory of assets to be divided according to the will. The inventory might identify stock holdings and other valuables bequeathed to him. He might still own these assets and they might easily be traced to him.

• When you were together, did you file joint tax returns that might disclose dividend income? You may be entitled to copies of those returns from the tax preparer.

• Did you and the father jointly purchase stocks, mutual funds, IRAs or other securities that you might be able to target. Perhaps you may remember signing your name to such related documents, but aren't sure exactly what they were. You may be able to insist that you have a right to examine the assets involved to determine whether you can legally pursue them. There may be brokerage and other records to look at.

• Do you know of any loans he applied for, including mortgages or other promissory notes, such as a car loan? If you were a co-signer of the note, you could ask to see the application.

CARS, BOATS AND PLANES

In most states, the public has a right to examine and get copies of documents listing vehicles owned by a person or firm. These records, usually maintained by the state's motor vehicle registry, commonly list the make, model, and year of each car, truck, van or motorcycle and the owner and his address.

They also list the vehicle identification number (VIN), which is stamped on the car. It is unique, like a fingerprint, in identifying a vehicle. Also recorded is the number of the license plate assigned to the vehicle. The records often list liens against the vehicle, usually reflecting a loan taken out to buy the car or truck. The lender is often identified.

To get this information, you must request it by mail and pay a fee. You have to be able to reasonably identify the person whose vehicle listing you want checked. Supply the person's full name, including middle initial, address, date of birth and Social Security number so that the state agency can make a good search.

If personal property taxes are levied in your county, the assessor's office probably would have a record of vehicles owned by residents in the county. The records may also show who owns mobile homes, boat and planes.

In some states, the same agency that registers cars and trucks also handles registration of most boats. **The Coast Guard registers yachts and other large boats.**

You can find if your ex-spouse owns a boat the same way you would inquire about vehicles he owns. The records would show when he acquired the boat, the price paid, the prior owner, the boat's description and identification number, and whether a loan was involved.

One of the authors once traced a cabin cruiser owned by a fun-loving state legislator charged with federal drug violations. The legislator was accused of handing out drugs during parties on the boat. Reporters tried to find the name of the boat, its registration, ownership and financing, but with no luck. The boat hadn't been registered with the Coast Guard and bore no state identification. But, unknown to the legislator, his name turned up as the owner in loan records filed by the lender with the state's Uniform Commercial Code section.

As in the case of cars and boats, some counties keep a record of airplane ownership for tax purposes. You may want to check the local airport to see if the absent dad keeps a plane there. If he has a pilot's license, or owns a plane, you can write to the Federal Aviation Administration and ask the agency to search its files.

The FAA handles the licensing of planes and pilots. You will need to supply the agency with enough personal data on your ex-spouse for it to make an effective search. The FAA can provide you with a listing of any aircraft he may own. It can also provide the address where a plane is registered to, the registration number, the plane's year and make, the insurance carrier, and information on the sale and previous owners. Inquiries may be directed to the FAA in Oklahoma City.

JEWELRY, FURNISHINGS, OTHER PERSONAL PROPERTY

If your missing dad bought jewelry, paintings, rare coins, and expensive furnishings it created a paper trial. He might be careless enough to leave receipts or sales slips lying around in drawers or other places. But he probably would not make it that easy for you to track these assets and make a legal claim against them. These must have enough value to warrant asking the court to issue a judgment against them and you may need an attorney to pursue it.

One way to check on an ex-spouse's buying habits is to go to your circuit court clerk's office and ask for help in checking all cases in which he was sued or sued someone. Perhaps some disgruntled merchant filed suit against him for failure to pay. It may pay you to also check records in the small claims court.

Depending on what state you live in, you can check records in the county collector's or assessor's office to see what personal property was included in his tax assessment. Some states limit the taxable personal property to vehicles, boats and planes. Other states tax valuables such as jewelry or items squirreled away in safe deposit boxes.

A check with the insurance company or agent used by you and your former spouse could turn up some surprises. Maybe he insured some valuables that you didn't know he had, like a house or car. A good source for finding out what valuables he has purchased is the credit card. Did you both once share a card that he used to buy expensive items without you being aware of it? If you both were owners of the credit card, you may be able to ask the company for a record of past purchases.

You should make an effort to examine his credit report to check for assets he may have acquired when you were together. Some mothers have been known to ask friendly business owners to run credit checks on the deadbeat dad after he left the family.

You may discover some expensive purchases buried in checking accounts that you jointly used, but which you never got to examine while you were together. Ask the bank to provide copies of monthly statements and then request copies of those checks that pique your interest.

Loompanics Unlimited, of Port Townsend, Wash., has published a manual for financial investigators titled, "How To Determine Undisclosed Financial Interests." It says that banks must keep for at least a two-year period all records needed to trace or describe a check of more than $100 deposited in a demand account.

The manual notes that most banks microfilm all checks, front and back, regardless of the amount since they have found it is cheaper to do so rather than incur the expense of sorting out those of lesser amounts.

OWNERSHIP IN BUSINESSES

If your ex-spouse owns a business, or is a partner or partial owner of a company, his stake is a potential asset that could benefit your children. How do you confirm his ownership interest?

One way might be to check the company's incorporation papers and annual reports on file with the state. Such records are often in the secretary of state's office. They list the persons who formed the company as well as the names of officers and directors.

It is possible to conceal the real ownership in such records, but on occasion the owners' names emerge in cases where votes are taken to amend the bylaws or change some of the provisions in the firm's scope of operations. In some states, you can find out the names of stockholders in publicly-traded companies by buying shares and asking to see the list of stockholders.

Other records that might tip you off to ownership could include municipal or state business permits or occupancy permits. Don't forget the faithful mail carriers who might tell you the names of people living at a specific address.

Property records may show who owns the property where your ex-spouse operates a business. They may also show if he has invested in limited real-estate partnerships or similar business ventures, and what assets he may have pledged as collateral.

While searching for collateral, ask for copies of any UCC (Uniform Commercial Code) filings that bear his name or his firm's name. These filings are made by lenders to protect themselves against default by the borrower or in litigation. They list loans they made to the person or company involved, along with the collateral that they required be put up by the borrower.

For example, a newspaper publisher might get a multi-million dollar loan for a printing press or other purposes. The lender makes a record of the loan and collateral with the state and county through a UCC filing to protect his interests and advise others of the existence of the debt. **The collateral might include real estate, securities or even a diamond necklace.**

Or an appliance company may use a UCC filing to record an installment loan granted for the purchase of a washing machine or refrigerator. The appliance itself could be the collateral, with the UCC filing serving as a public notice of the debt.

One investigative reporter used UCC records to expose corruption by a Chicago alderman. Ed Pound, then with the Chicago Sun-Times, documented secret land dealings by the alderman which led to his conviction and five-year federal prison sentence. How Pound did it was described in the book, *Investigative Reporting And Editing,* by the late Paul N. Williams.

Williams wrote that Pound figured out how to trace secret trusts through which the alderman owned land that benefitted from city council actions he arranged. The trusts were set up in such a way that they concealed the true ownership.

By examining UCC files, Pound learned that banks that loaned the alderman sizeable amounts had recorded the transactions in the UCC section of the secretary of state's office. The listings of the alderman's collateral showed some of the secret trusts among his assets. Pound was then able to link the land dealings to the alderman's actions on the city council.

Another source of information on the finances of a company and its key personnel can be found in the files of the Securities and Exchange Commission (SEC). Under SEC rules, any company with more than 500 stockholders and more than $1 million in assets is required to make a public annual report to its stockholders.

Some of the more important SEC reports, available either in Washington or regional SEC offices, include Form 3, the so-called insider report. It requires that any officer, director, or person holding more than 10 percent of a company's registered securities must file a report with the agency listing his or her "beneficial ownership" of stock. Reports also must be filed for any month in which there was a change in their holdings.

Form S-1 is well worth examining. This is the registration form for companies first coming under SEC jurisdiction. It includes the personal and business histories of officers, along with the firm's capital structure and lines of credit.

Companies selling stock to the public also file Form 10-K annually with the SEC. This report includes descriptions of property owned by the firm, organizational structure and the names and backgrounds of top officers and directors. It also lists major lawsuits pending. Another report, Form 8-K, lists changes in a company's ownership, assets or finances. People acquiring 5 percent or more of a company's stock are listed in Form 13-D.

But often, you don't need to turn to federal records to find out about your ex-spouse's holdings or income in a business. If he's made enemies within the company, his present or former associates might be willing to tell you about his financial affairs and assets.

INCOME AND EARNINGS

Before you can get child support, the court has to know how much money the children's father is able to pay. The enforcement agency has access to state employment records and also combined federal-state computerized directories showing every person newly-hired by every employer in the country so federal and state investigators can track down deadbeats, especially those who cross state lines.

But some enforcement agencies are notoriously inept at locating a non-payor. That's why it's important that you know, or find, where he is employed and how much he's earning. You may have to be the one to provide this information to child support enforcement officials.

If the employer is verified, part of his pay can be attached by the court if he fails to keep up with his court-ordered child support payments.

You may know your ex's line of work, but not who employs him or how much he earns. If he is a union worker, you may be able to learn what his hourly wage and benefits are under a contract negotiated by the union with his employer. The union contract usually tells what the general wage rates are for the type of work he is doing.

If you suspect who his employer is, but are not positive, try calling the company's personnel office and say: "I want to verify employment for (give his name)." Companies usually will cooperate on such requests if they believe the employee has applied to rent a home or apartment or has applied for a loan or credit.

Some mothers have pretended to be calling from a rental firm or lending institution. Others have used friendly business owners to make the call. After verifying with a company that an ex-spouse works there, some women go a step further and ask what his weekly or monthly salary is, saying: "I need to confirm the information."

If your ex-spouse is a public employee you ought to be able to find out how much he earns by asking the agency that employs him. If the agency refuses to tell you, you can ask to see its payroll. You may have to request it under the state's Freedom of Information Act. Your caseworker can formally request a record of his earnings.

17

GETTING THE MONEY

WAYS TO GO AFTER HIS INCOME AND ASSETS

Now that you've located him and identified his earnings and assets, it's time to move on them. There are legal steps that can be taken to force your ex-partner to pay the support he owes.

State and federal laws require him to pay. So it's not just you getting on his case. It's the whole child-support enforcement system, including caseworkers, prosecutors and judges. Activist groups such as ACES will give moral support and advice on how to collect.

As you pursue your deadbeat dad, keep an exact record of every penny he has paid and hasn't paid, along with the dates. The best system is when all child-support payments go through the circuit clerk, or appropriate official, so a permanent record of all payments is made. This will help eliminate payment disputes down the road.

If he's paying you directly for some reason, make copies of any checks. Be wary of taking cash. List it in your record of payments, give him a receipt for it, and ask him to sign your copy of the receipt.

A custodial mother may need legal help in going after unpaid support.

The best approach is to get the CSE agency to work with a government lawyer or prosecutor responsible for enforcing collections. Of course, you must ask the agency to open a case file.

Or you can retain a lawyer to collect support. Many private attorneys handle child-support collection cases on a contingency fee basis. You may or may not have to pay up-front money. The law firm may take up to one third of the total payments it collects.

Some county and state agencies don't like working with private attorneys to collect support. They feel that if a woman can hire an attorney she doesn't need or want the state's help. It may also cause conflicts on making enforcement decisions.

Listed below are some collection strategies. We'll discuss each one individually. Some of these methods can be used by the CSE office.

- Wage Withholding
- Interstate Collecting
- Dogging Him If He Works For Cash
- Seizing His Assets
- Slapping A Lien On Him
- Getting A Withhold and Deliver Order
- Getting Children's Medical Support
- Modifying Support Orders
- Threatening Prosecution
- Yanking His Professional License
- Reporting Him To Credit Bureaus
- If He Dies, Get What's Left

WAGE WITHHOLDING

When the dad doesn't make voluntary support payments, wage withholding is the most effective way for a woman to get him to pay regularly. Skipped or delayed payments can disrupt the family's life. That's why Congress several years ago mandated that immediate wage withholding be included in all court orders, unless both parents agree to another plan.

Interstate wage withholding can be used to enforce support in another state where the dad's employer is known. States are required to honor and continue wage withholding orders from other states. Older child-support orders can be revised to include wage withholding. If the noncustodial parent is regularly employed, a portion of his earnings can be withheld for child support, just like other forms of payroll deductions.

Federal law requires employers — regardless of size — to cooperate in withholding. Some fail to do it because they are unaware of the law. The law also says that in the case of older support orders, wage withholding can be triggered when the father or mother is at least one month behind in paying. States can apply withholding to other forms of income besides wages. These may include bonuses, commissions, retirement benefits, rental or interest income, unemployment benefits, Social Security and military retirement pay. Wage withholding can be used for both ongoing support and arrearages.

A custodial mother can have her own attorney work to collect support payments through wage withholding. Critics say this approach takes away some of the money owed to the children. Or, the attorney can work with the child-support enforcement program to coordinate the collection.

Once a support order is issued with a provision for wage withholding, the money can be paid directly to the mother by the father. As mentioned earlier, the better method is to have it paid into the court system for record-keeping and distribution.

All federal civilian employees are subject to wage withholding. You can also seek garnishment of wages of active, reserve and retired members of the military with the assistance of your caseworker or lawyer. You can seek a garnishment order from the court and send it with a certified copy of your child-support order to the designated military official.

If a self-employed deadbeat has incorporated his own company, wage withholding can be used to collect child support. It the company fails to pay, it can be held liable for the money. Civil court remedies can include placing the deadbeat's company in receivership, but this is rare at best. An appointed trustee would be required to pay the company's debts, with priority given to child support.

INTERSTATE COLLECTING

One of the toughest problems is when a parent in one state tries to collect child support from an ex-spouse who has moved to another state. In cases where there are court orders for support, all states are required by federal law to work as diligently for children who live outside their borders as for those under their own jurisdiction. But for thousands of families, it doesn't happen. Getting officials in the two states to work together can turn into a time-consuming and frustrating experience. The states are self-governing, having different laws, court systems and "good old boy" practices.

Too many cases fall between the cracks because of huge caseloads, lack of resources, poor tracking of cases, and bureaucratic indifference. As mentioned previously, interstate wage withholding can be used when the non-custodial parent's employer is known. It can save weeks of waiting for court dates. The child-support enforcement office in the state where the deadbeat parent is living should make sure that a wage withholding order contains all the information required.

States have laws that require them to refer cases to other states. One is called URESA (Uniform Reciprocal Enforcement of Support Act). A newer law is UIFSA (Uniform Interstate Family Support Act). Both include procedures for an official or a private attorney to seek a filing in another state.

When a dad is transferred by his company to another state, federal law requires the new state to recognize a wage-withholding order from the other state. The new state must continue the wage-withhold order as written — regardless of where the custodial parent and children may live. If the dad has moved to another country, you can try to get your court order enforced by your state CSE office, which may have an agreement with the foreign country. If he works for a company with offices in the United States, wage withholding might work, officials say.

It is a federal offense for someone to willfully fail to pay past due support for a child living in another state. Although it's usually treated as a misdemeanor, the FBI gets involved and the feds seldom lose a case. In some states, non-support violations are felonies. States are supposed to report to federal prosecutors cases of deadbeats who have crossed state lines to avoid paying.

In recent years, the U.S. Justice Department has directed U.S. attorneys nationwide to increase the number of prosecutions. Some of the flagrant cases that involved wealthy men who owed large sums of support have been played up by the news media.

DOGGING HIM IF HE WORKS FOR CASH

Collecting child support from fathers or mothers who are self-employed can be difficult if they don't want to cooperate. The same is true if they work for cash or commissions. They may be dead-set against paying anything to their former partners and use deception to hide their income. They try to rationalize their irresponsible and selfish behavior by blaming it on the other person. They cheat their own kids and think it's OK.

What can child-support enforcement officials do in such cases? They can use tactics to increase pressure to make him pay. The Handbook on Child Support Enforcement suggests one scenario:

At first, the CSE (Child Support Enforcement) office should encourage voluntary payment by monthly billings or telephone reminders. Some CSE offices send out delinquency notices or use mailgrams to elicit regular payments. Check to see if this is being done for your case.

Other techniques include attaching real and personal property or assets, credit bureau reporting, intercepting state and federal tax refunds, placing liens on his property or garnishing his bank account.

If he still refuses to pay, a judgment can be sought to enforce the child support order. You have the right to seek a judgment to enforce the child support order. You should work through your caseworker or local prosecutor to get the judgment. A warrant for his arrest can then be issued.

But getting police or sheriff's deputies to make such arrests can be a chore. They claim they have other priorities. Some mothers have gotten action only after telling police where and when to find the deadbeat. Others threaten to complain to the news media, or do, to get the system moving.

SEIZING HIS ASSETS

States can play hardball to convince deadbeat dads to pay.

They can seize federal and state income tax refunds in cases where a father ignores support orders and is in arrears.

Under federal law, states that impose a state income tax must take from the refund an amount of money to satisfy past-due child support. This applies to both welfare and non-welfare mothers.

The state must notify the noncustodial parent in advance of taking the action. The notice specifies the amount owed in arrears and the amount to be offset. It also tells who the dad should contact to contest the offset.

States can ask the IRS to intercept federal refunds when past-due support owed to non-welfare mothers exceeds $500, or $150 in the case of welfare recipients.

To be eligible for a state or federal tax offset, you must have a legal order for child support that spells out the amount your ex-spouse is obligated to pay, and how it is to be paid.

If a delinquent dad is lucky enough to win a state lottery, let's hope it's in one of the states that have been seizing portions of lottery winnings from deadbeat dads.

The state may be able to seize and sell his property, with the proceeds applied to his support debt. This is assuming that he has the property in his name alone, and does not have a lien.

SLAPPING HIM WITH LIENS

Together with your attorney or a CSE lawyer, you may be able to place liens on real or personal property owned by the father. This could prevent him from selling the property or borrowing against it, without first satisfying the child support debt. Usually a *lis pendens* can be filed with the recorder of deeds to alert interested parties that a legal action is pending.

Getting a lien placed doesn't by itself force payment, but it may encourage the non-custodial dad to pay up so he can retain clear title to the property. There's a catch. Most states will not put a lien on a primary residence or attach property such as a car that the delinquent parent needs to make a living. But the father who owes child support may be hard put to justify keeping other vehicles he owns from being attached.

Mothers should consult their caseworkers, or attorneys, about what kinds of property are available for liens or attachment in their state.

WITHHOLD AND DELIVER

Under some state laws, the enforcement official can issue an order to "withhold and deliver" certain assets if the dad is in arrears. The order is sent to any person, company or institution holding property belonging to the debtor, such as bank accounts, investments, second homes, second cars and other personal property.

The holder of the property must deliver it either to the mother, sheriff or enforcement agency, or to the court that issued the support order.

Deadbeats with poor payment history can also be forced to post security, bond, property or other guarantee to the court as a pledge that support will be paid. Such collateral could be forfeited if payment isn't made.

MEDICAL SUPPORT

Your support order should require the father to have medical insurance coverage for your children. This should be part of a divorce decree or separation order. If it is not in the court order, or you do not have an order, apply for the medical coverage through your CSE agency.

The agency must petition the court to include medical support in any order for child support when group health insurance is available to the father through his job, or at a reasonable cost. This would allow your children to be covered under their dad's health plan even though he hasn't enrolled them.

Existing court orders can be modified to include health coverage for your children. You can hire an attorney to help get medical support, or you can represent yourself in court. In some states the dad gets credit for his cost on maintaining medical insurance for the children and this amount may be deducted from his monthly support payment.

Federal law requires states to make medical support enforcement easier. Insurers can no longer refuse to enroll a child in a parent's health care plan because the parents were not married or because the child does not live in the same household as the enrolled parent, or have the same last name. Health insurers, as well as employers, are required to comply with medical support provisions of CS orders and to assist in their enforcement.

All federal agencies, including the military, have been directed by presidential order to cooperate fully in efforts to establish paternity and child support orders. They must enforce the collection of child support and medical support.

MODIFYING SUPPORT ORDERS

If your support is inadequate, or your ex's income has increased, it's up to you to ask for a judge to modify the support order to provide more money. You will have to provide information on your finances, as well as details of the dad's income and assets. The father has to be notified of the request.

A caveat: Filing a motion to increase your support may open the door to his filing a cross-motion asking the court to grant him custody or increased visitation rights.

If your ex-spouse remarries, and has other children to support, this does not excuse him from paying support to the children he had with you. He's still responsible. But in some cases, judges have granted the dad a decrease in the child support he must pay to his first family because of the needs of his new family. You should be given advance notice so you can contest any reduction. CSE offices review child support orders every three years if the family is receiving welfare. Non-welfare cases may be reviewed every three years if either parent requests it — or more often at the state's option. Ask your caseworker about doing a review and modifying the support order if needed.

Tell your caseworker immediately if you learn about any change in the father's employment situation. It could help in attaching his wages, or if he's out of work, in attaching his unemployment compensation. If the mother remarries and her new husband adopts her child, the child's biological father can seek an end to support payments. He'll still owe back support.

If your child is over 18 and is due back support, you may be able to recover it. Check to see if your state is among those that requires an arrearage to be paid to a child who is no longer a minor.

In some states, the non-custodial parent is required to continue paying support to disabled children over 18 years of age. In some states, child support must be paid for children in college. And in some states children who reach legal age are entitled to collect back support.

Child support generally cannot be discharged in bankruptcy. A parent who owes child support cannot escape his duty by filing for bankruptcy. The issue is complicated and you may want to seek legal guidance.

THREATENING PROSECUTION

With the growing number of parents refusing to pay child support, state and federal lawmakers have imposed stricter criminal penalties for chronic deadbeats who have the ability to pay. Some states have made it a felony to be in arrears for certain amounts over a period of time.

It's usually up to the local prosecutor on how tough the law will be applied. Prosecutors who seek re-election usually want to win favor with female voters by getting publicity on prosecuting deadbeat dads.

But some prosecutors feel it's counter-productive to put a deadbeat in jail, thereby preventing him from earning money that can be used for child support payments. A counter argument is that the threat of jail may get him to begin paying.

Some mothers whose cases have been ignored have used the local news media to spotlight their plight and get action from the local CSE agency or prosecutor.

For several years federal prosecutors did little to enforce a 1992 law making it a federal crime for a person not to pay child support for a child living in another state. But in recent years, prodded by Congress, prosecutors have been instructed by the Attorney General to go after more interstate deadbeats. The feds now make sure they get publicity when they catch a big fish, such as a millionaire deadbeat. It makes the administration look good at election time.

If your case is an interstate one, the CSE agency can refer it to the U.S. Attorney's office. Or you can go directly to the federal prosecutor's office and ask it to take your case. It must meet three criteria: the deadbeat parent lives in a different state than the child; he is at least one year, or $5,000, in arrears; and he has willfully failed to pay support. The government must prove that he had the ability to pay.

YANKING HIS PROFESSIONAL LICENSE

In cases where a deadbeat holds a professional license, pressure can be added by asking state licensing authorities to revoke or suspend his license for repeatedly violating the support order. More states are taking such steps because they realize that deadbeat dads who can afford to pay, but refuse, are pushing their children onto welfare rolls.

California was a leader in the movement, lifting licenses of doctors, lawyers, engineers and many other professionals for failing to pay support.

REPORT DEADBEAT TO CREDIT BUREAUS

If he's a chronic deadbeat, urge your enforcement workers to report him to credit bureaus for not paying his obligations. This will hurt his ability to get loans or credit cards.

By law, CSE offices must report child support arrearages of over $1,000 (or less at the state's option) to credit bureaus. The state notifies the non-custodial parent that the overdue debt will be reported to the credit reporting network. That sometimes is enough to encourage him to pay up.

See if you can later check the dad's credit report to see if you are listed as a creditor. You may well have a legal right to see the credit report. Seek counsel from your own attorney or an attorney for the child-support enforcement agency.

IF HE DIES, GET WHAT'S LEFT

If the children's father dies, his children should be entitled to their share of any assets he leaves.

A well-written child support order should define child support payments as a claim against his estate.

The order should provide that his children be named as beneficiaries in his will, life insurance policies, pension funds, retirement plan, securities and property.

After 10 Years Of No Support, She Hires A Pro, Gets $37,000

During the nearly 10 years that her ex-husband failed to pay child support, Nancy Sissons had to go to work at two jobs in order to provide support for her two daughters.

Sissons

She got payments for a year after they were separated. "We got divorced in 1983. Right after that, it stopped," said Sissons, of Glen Cove, Long Island, N.Y.

Her ex-husband, a mechanical engineer, was moving around the country. She had little hope of ever seeing another dollar from him. She worked full time in an office at a university and did waitressing five nights a week.

"It was a difficult time in my life," Sissons says. "I just remember going from one job to the other, and always being very tired. I didn't have a choice — it was something I had to do."

She recalls repeated visits or telephone calls to child support workers and always being told they hadn't yet located her ex. She kept a 6-inch-thick personal folder.

"I had filed with Nassau County but that went on for nine years and I got nothing," she said. "A woman in the Nassau office told me I might as well forget it."

A friend in Texas who knew of her problem told her about an Austin-based firm run by Casey Hoffman that helped a bank teller get her child support. Sissons wrote to Hoffman. "I had nothing to lose," she said.

Then came the surprise. "Within three days they called to say they had located him," she said. He had been in Florida, California and Texas.

Her ex-husband ended up paying $37,000, and after Hoffman's fee, Sissons got about $25,000. "I can't say enough kind things about him (Hoffman)," she said.

Upon getting her ex's address, her older daughter wrote to him.

After an absence of 12 years, "She got a birthday card from him and they are keeping in touch," Sissons said.

Hoffman later cited Sissons' case when he testified before a congressional committee investigating child support collection problems.

18

SHOULD YOU HIRE OUTSIDE HELP TO COLLECT?

THE PROS AND CONS

Richard "Casey" Hoffman makes no apology for taking one third of the child support money that he collects for women who come to his firm:

"They've been without child support for years and the government didn't help them. They've got no more money for lawyers. They look upon us as a godsend rather than someone taking advantage of the situation."

Hoffman left his job as director of the Texas child support agency in 1990 to start his own firm to help custodial parents collect unpaid child support. The Austin-based firm — Child Support Enforcement *CSE — is now one of the nation's largest private collectors for child support.

"We make a difference in the lives of children," Hoffman said. Private collection firms can help the children, the custodial parents and taxpayers, he said. "If child support is paid, they can stay off welfare, in some cases. Each case we do is one less for the government to do.

"Over 90 percent of our clients have already gone through the government collection system and haven't been helped." Hoffman said his company collects in 58 percent of it cases — three times the average chalked up by states nationwide.

A growing number of frustrated mothers have turned to dozens of debt-collection agencies nationwide to get their child support. The firms work on a contingency basis and are selective in who they will take on as a client. They usually turn down welfare cases because most of the money collected would go to repay the state for welfare payments.

They focus on cases where clients already have a court order and are owed at least several thousand dollars in back support. They have the client sign a contract spelling out what their fee will be. The firms take a big bite, often one-third of what they collect. But some moms feel it's worth getting something, rather than nothing.

PRIVATE COLLECTORS THRIVE WHEN GOVERNMENT FAILS

Private collection agencies first began pursuing deadbeat dads on a large scale in the late 1980's when so many single parents lost faith that the child support system was working for them.

Bill collectors who were experts in chasing down delinquent car payments and credit card debts found a profitable new field in tracking deadbeat dads across the nation who owed billions of dollars in back support. Some collectors discovered all they needed was a telephone and a willingness to harass their prey.

The private firms' investigators include former cops, child support enforcement workers, skip tracers and even repo men. They can tap into credit bureaus, computer databases and other files. They tell deadbeats to pay up or risk having liens placed on their property, wages garnished, their professional licenses revoked, or being arrested on outstanding warrants.

Critics of the debt collectors say the states already have collection systems and mothers shouldn't have to go to the private sector and give up so much of their children's support.

Geraldine Jensen, a child-support activist, calls collectors "vultures" who prey on vulnerable mothers and children. "We need to fix the system, not let private companies profit at the expense of kids," she was quoted by the New York Times.

To complicate matters, one third of the states are using collection agencies themselves.

In hiring a collection agency you should have a clear understanding of what services will be provided and the cost. The charge could be a percentage of what's collected, or be based on an hourly charge, with no guarantee of success. A private attorney might request a retainer up front and charge a set percentage of any back child support money collected.

Some collection firms charge an initial fee of about $40 or more, along with taking up to a third of any support money they collect. Hoffman said some collectors charge fees and don't perform the work.

"I would caution every person to investigate carefully the company and not pay application fees," Hoffman said. "Any legitimate provider of child support enforcement services ought to be able to take the risk and not charge any money up front." He said that because many private firms aren't subject to regulatory overview, parents should consider using collection agencies headed by lawyers who must answer to their state bar associations.

A FEW FLY-BY-NIGHT FIRMS GO BUST

This happened in a St. Louis suburb where the owner of a defunct collection agency pleaded guilty to bilking clients out of thousands of dollars. Complaints had poured in from about 50 women whose checks bounced or never arrived. They found their collector, who they had given the power of attorney to receive wage assignments from employers, was a bigger deadbeat than their ex-spouses.

Private collection firms work with custodial parents who have court orders for child support but are owed thousands of dollars in back support. The client must sign a contract giving the firm power of attorney.

"That allows us to get any records relating to their case within the court system," Hoffman explained. "We are trying to gather all the evidence of what is owed. We have the right to have an attorney represent the client and do wage withholding, ask for license revocation, place liens on property, move for contempt proceedings and find if there are any arrest warrants outstanding."

The check for the arrearage may be made out to the mother, the state or the collecting agency, depending on the court order. The payment is recorded by the court system to document the amount of back support paid.

Hoffman and other private collectors say that because they work on contingency, if they don't collect support money, they don't get paid. But government enforcement workers can fail to collect, without penalty.

TIPS FROM CASEY HOFFMAN:

Custodial parents who want to use a private company to collect support should:

- Avoid companies that charge up-front application fees.
- Make sure the company is bonded and distributes child support immediately.
- Read any contract carefully before signing. Make sure it mentions the specific amount of money the firm is to collect and the time it has to do it.
- Be certain of what percentage the company takes for its efforts.
- Ask for a list of other clients and talk to them.
- Check with the Better Business Bureau.
- Ask questions on how the company operates and the expertise of its officers.

From CS Bureaucrat To Hired Gun

As Casey Hoffman was growing up in Massachusetts, the talk around the dinner table often was about problems affecting families. "My dad was a family law judge and mom was an activist in women's issues," he said.

Hoffman

He became a family law attorney, had a stint as a prosecutor, and later was appointed to the Massachusetts Child Support Commission. In 1985, he moved to Texas to become director of the state's child-support program, one of the largest in the country.

When he left that job five years later, the Texas program was rated the most improved in the nation. And Hoffman was named the outstanding child-support manager of the year.

He quit to start his own collection firm. "It was time to go off and try to realize the vision I had — to complement the government and help win the child support war," Hoffman said. "I enjoyed my government service, but I wanted to design a program that would solve the problem."

Hoffman testified before Congress that there are 15 million cases in which no child support has been paid. He said the No. 1 reason is an overwhelming backlog of cases in the government program.

"Dedicated workers run from one case to the next in a frenzy of activity, having to spend valuable time dealing with complaints, audits, new directions and computerization deadlines," he said.

Some call Hoffman a bounty hunter — a term he dislikes. Another term he dislikes, and won't use, is "deadbeat dad." He said he doesn't want to make child support a sexist fight.

"The bottom line is that there are three choices. One is the government. Two is using private attorneys. The third is companies like I have. I'm not against any one of these three," he said. "I ask myself what would I advise if I had a sister and she came to me with this problem."

PART 4
WHAT WILL IT TAKE TO HELP THE CHILDREN?

19

KIDS NEED CHAMPIONS

The travesty of unpaid child support should be a public issue of top priority. But it isn't.

Moms and their children, in poor economic straits, lack the political clout to influence changes in the child support system. They form no constituency and have few champions for their cause. Rather than being seen as victims, they are blamed for their own plight.

This social problem has been largely ignored by the news media, lawmakers and government bureaucrats.

Journalists will admit issues like the economy and health care get top coverage nationally but non-payment of child support gets little public attention. That's because it is seen mainly as a women-and-children issue.

Decisions affecting news coverage have traditionally been made by male editors and reporters. Few of them recognized the enormity of the child support problem. So too, with male-dominated law enforcement, courts, state legislatures and Congress. It's a gender thing.

Many educated and well-off women who could help, such as journalists and lawmakers, are preoccupied with their own careers. They pursue issues important to them, such as equal job and promotion opportunities, equal pay with men, family leave, gender bias, and sexual harassment. They don't relate to the woman who can't get her child support. It's a class thing.

NATIONAL ENQUIRER TARGETS DEADBEATS

Some newspapers, magazines and TV and radio stations have periodically exposed failures of the child support system. But for the most part, the problem is given only glancing attention — as though it was not worthy of a major investigative campaign. The National Enquirer is a notable exception.

Since 1992, The National Enquirer has crusaded steadily against some of the nation's worst deadbeat dads, publishing their photos and those of the families they abandoned.

Dozens have been depicted as fugitives who should be hunted down. Millions of the tabloid's readers are urged to join the manhunt. Those deadbeats caught are featured in follow-up stories.

John Blosser, writer of the series, said the response was greater than expected from readers, who are mostly women. He said some of the exposed deadbeats later became real parents, resuming support payments and visitation with their children. "Hopefully, we can affect the public awareness the way mothers did against drunk driving," Blosser said.

In one case, the Enquirer torpedoed one deadbeat's plans to "dump his 10 kids, stiff them for $71,000 in support, and sail off into the sunset on his 27-foot boat." It tracked the runaway dad from Alaska to St. Petersburg, Fla., where he was finally reeled in by authorities at a marina, the tabloid said. It credited a reader who "spotted the tanned 54-year-old sailor lounging on his boat....and called us."

One deadbeat, said to owe his daughter more than $70,000, was found years later, teaching golf in Japan. A tipster saw his name on a credit reference when the runaway dad bought a car. "We got a lucky break," Blosser said. As the man gave golf lessons, the Enquirer's photographer hid "in the bushes banging off pictures," he said. The story resulted in the man paying support.

GOVERNMENT'S SORRY RECORD

In 1974 Congress launched the child support enforcement system to reform what had been an ineffective state and local effort at collecting support. Since then — despite federal overview, and billions of dollars plowed into CS enforcement — the low collection rates among the states remain a travesty. And this directly harms the children who are supposed to be helped.

A person who receives a check that bounced has a far better chance of recouping the amount through a prosecutor than a single mom has in collecting unpaid support from a deadbeat dad.

The statistic of child support being collected in only one of five cases nationwide has remained constant in recent years. This helps explain why so many families have been forced to go on welfare.

Why is the record so sorry? A key reason is because state and local child support agencies have continued to do their own collections. Most have failed miserably. In a recent year the states with the worst records collected child support in only about 10 percent of their cases. The best states collected in about 40 percent of cases.

Some in Congress say real reform is long overdue and are calling for a major change in the collection system. One is Rep. Lynn Woolsey, D-Calif., who has co-sponsored a proposal to have the IRS handle all collections. Child support payments would be withheld from an absent father's paycheck the way taxes are.

"The states have had their chance to improve child support collection, but they have failed our children and bankrupted our welfare system....It is a national crisis demanding a national solution," Woolsey said.

Woolsey says the current system allows states and counties to ignore the mom who is owed child support and is barely making ends meet, but is not yet on welfare. "The system has nothing invested in helping her. We've got to prevent mothers like her from going on welfare."

ACES — A GRASSROOTS CHAMP

Single mothers struggling to raise their families without child support are truly champions for their kids. But many of those moms need an ally to turn to. If there is one group that has championed their cause it is the Association for Children for Enforcement of Support, called ACES.

The group was founded in 1984 in Toledo, Ohio, by Geraldine Jensen, who is president. It has more than 35,000 members — mostly women — in 350 chapters across the nation.

Besides helping custodial parents get child support, it conducts a public awareness campaign and presses for needed reforms at the state and federal levels. ACES faults state-based collection systems and favors having the IRS handle collections.

The ACES staff is aided by more than 4,500 volunteers from chapters across the country. Each year 100,000 families entitled to child support contact it for information. The group works with local and state agencies to help children get child support. To highlight the plight of abandoned children, it has staged candlelight vigils, sponsored seminars and filed lawsuits.

A snapshot of the average ACES member showed a single mother of two earning about $11,000 a year. She can't afford health insurance, can't pay the children's medical bills, or hire a private attorney to pursue back support. The system has failed her. About half the members are divorced or separated, while the others were never married to the father of their children.

ACES offers members a book, "How To Collect Child Support." Jensen is author of the book. ACES also publishes a newspaper three times a year, and provides information booklets and videos on various child support issues. For a minimal fee, it will do a computer search for a deadbeat parent. A search could turn up property, businesses or other assets owned by the delinquent parent. To reach ACES:

ACES National Headquarters

2260 Upton Avenue
Toledo, Ohio 43606
(419) 472-6609
(Hotline) 1-800-738-ACES (2237)

Tabloid Writer Pummels Deadbeat 'Bums'

John Blosser remembers his dad working in a West Virginia coal mine and then as a bread delivery man, getting up before daylight each day. For 25 years his dad supported his family without question or complaint.

Blosser

"That's my model of what a man is. A man takes care of business and his responsibilities," Blosser said.

That's why he feels little sympathy for deadbeat dads and their excuses. He's tracked them for years while doing exposés in the National Enquirer. If you're a deadbeat, and Blosser gets you in his cross-hairs, it will be your worst nightmare. You'll be pilloried in headlines read by millions.

You'll be called a jerk, scum, heartless bum, creep, sleaze, scoundrel, callous rat or cruel louse. Other publications shy away from such name-calling. But Blosser says, "We call them bums because that's what they are."

"What angers me is the way these guys drop out of their kids' lives," Blosser says. "The emotional harm is horrible. The children lose both parents when the mom has to go to work." He believes failure to pay child support is child abuse.

"I hope we're doing some good," says Blosser, the senior reporter who helped create the National Enquirer series. He says he's heard every excuse from deadbeats. He tells them: "If you can't feed 'em, don't breed 'em."

Blosser says the problem is "too large to be solved through the government or courts. You're not going to solve this thing until you change the way people think" about dads who don't pay.

BLOSSER SAYS RAISE HELL WHEN YOU CAN'T GET HELP

In getting child support, "In the end, women have to do it for themselves," says National Enquirer writer John Blosser. He offers these tips to mothers who call him:

• Raise hell when you get no help from the CSE workers. "You have to become the biggest pain in the butt they have ever seen. If they complain about you calling every other day, start calling every day. Call the governor. Call the FBI. Call anyone you can think of."

• "Put his face on a wanted poster and make 500 copies of it. Put it on trees, at his office, or wherever. Turn his life into a living hell."

• Go to the news media. If your story gets publicized, it puts a fire under the CSE officials.

• If you use a bounty hunter or collection agency don't pay them up front. "They may charge $200 or so, up front, and never do anything. Some take only the easy cases."

• Give the deadbeat a chance to shape up. "Some are not bad guys necessarily. They get themselves in a bind, build up a big debt, and they take off." If they can't make the payments, some will negotiate and try to pay some support, and keep in contact with their children.

20

THERE HAS TO BE A BETTER WAY

THE SYSTEM IS BROKEN, BUT IT DOESN'T GET FIXED.

Government spends $3 billion a year on the child support system nation-wide, but collections are made in only one of every five cases.

Some $40 billion is owed by deadbeat parents to children in about 11 million families. The government doesn't report how many kids are owed support, but ACES puts the number at about 30 million.

While there are many problems with the system, the overall collection rate remains pathetic, pushing about half the kids in single-parent homes onto welfare.

IS IRS THE ANSWER?

Boosting collections is the main issue. Some reformers — who have given up hope on ever having the states do a better job — are pushing for the IRS to take over the collections. It would be done through withholding of child support obligations from wages, just as taxes and Social Security are withheld.

"We need to federalize support enforcement," says **U.S. Rep. Henry Hyde, R-Ill.** He and **U.S. Rep. Lynn Woolsey, D-CA.,** co-sponsored a bill to do just that. "The IRS is the one governmental agency that has the reputation and the statutory resources needed to make good on this country's promise to custodial parents that they will get their children support, at an affordable cost to us all," Hyde said.

Hyde

To many, using the IRS is an appealing remedy. It's sort of a last-resort effort to combat persistent social problems and poverty caused largely by non-payment of support. With welfare cutbacks, single mothers and their kids need their child support more than ever.

And deadbeat dads would get the message that they better not mess with the IRS. The IRS plan wouldn't catch up with all the deadbeats. But proponents say it would immediately remove several hundred thousand children from the welfare rolls. Also, they argue, the IRS would do a better job in collecting from deadbeats who flee to other states.

Yet the bills in Congress to transfer collections to the IRS encountered rough sailing. Some lawmakers are wary of the tax agency, partly because of disclosures of horrific abuses toward taxpayers. A survey by the authors of state directors of child support enforcement agencies showed most of those responding were against having the IRS do the collections. One refrain was that they didn't think the IRS could do a better job.

Some of the opponents may be jealous over turf and fear losing their positions, say backers of transferring the collection function to the IRS. They say the states would still establish paternity, get child support orders, set awards, and work with families.

CHRONIC FLAWS: WILL SOMEBODY DO SOMETHING?

Barbara Grob, director of the San Francisco-based Child Support Reform Initiative, says regardless of who makes collections, there are other reforms needed. She cites these:

- Simplify hospital procedures for establishing paternity.
- Streamline processes for setting awards.
- Make award guidelines more uniform and adequate.
- Make employee withholding more routine.
- Take steps to handle the ever-growing caseloads.
- Toughen enforcement on non-payors.

There's no great pressure to reform the child support system, Grob said. "The public has very little knowledge of the harm nonpayment of child support does to children," she said.

Grob says there needs to be a change in the climate that tolerates widespread refusal to pay child support.

HUGE CASELOADS

The flood of child support cases has overwhelmed the state Child Support Enforcement agencies. Statistics in a recent year show that child support wasn't collected in more than 15 million of the nation's 19 million cases.

State officials responding to our survey said they lacked the staff and funding to cope with the caseloads. For women seeking child support, it could take years to get their cases worked on. Most just give up.

In Texas, the attorney general's office said "escalating births, coupled with a steady divorce rate, have pushed caseloads beyond the means of most child support agencies. And, until these agencies receive the necessary funding to handle the workload, collections are going to suffer."

"In Maryland," an official replied, "the child support collection system has suffered from a judicial process which involved overburdened court systems and extensive paperwork. Adding to that, for a number of years our metropolitan offices operated under overwhelmingly large caseloads."

New Mexico's reply: "Ninety percent of people on welfare are there because someone is not paying child support. By having a workable caseload most could be removed from the welfare rolls."

Casey Hoffman, former head of Texas' child support program, says the average caseload in the country is 1,000 cases per worker. He told a congressional subcommittee that caseworkers "run from one case to the next in a frenzy."

Hoffman suggested: "first, work the cases on welfare and then the ones where the families may very well end up on welfare if you don't collect the child support owed."

GET THOSE COMPUTERS WORKING!

Geraldine Jensen, president of ACES, says the computer network that the states were supposed to set up to talk to each other and track absent parents has been a costly failure.

The federal government gave the states $2.6 billion for computers but most of them could not meet federal guidelines or deadlines. ACES found that many child support files are outdated and inaccurate.

Eight states not likely to get their computer systems in line represented nearly 50 percent of the nation's child support cases, ACES said. One of them, California, had to scrap its system altogether and begin over.

"We need a modern, efficient national computer system to locate absent parents. This cannot be the statewide computer systems tied together," ACES said in a report.

What is needed, ACES said, is a national locator system run by the IRS. This would protect confidential records far better than in the state and local systems.

ASSURING EACH CHILD

Irwin Garfinkel, authority on child poverty, is a leading advocate of having the government guarantee each child a minimum support level. Such a "child support assurance system" would provide a payment to families to make up the difference when court-ordered child support is not fully paid.

Garfinkel says divorces and out-of-wedlock childbirths are rising so fast that over half of the next generation is likely to be raised in single-mother families. And as many as half of these families will live in poverty, he said.

ACES also backs a child support assurance program. It notes that some states have already adopted such programs. Says ACES: "Unlike welfare, the assurance program does not decrease when the custodial parent takes a job, earns more money, or marries."

The child support assurance idea is favored by other child advocacy groups such the Child Support Reform Initiative and the Center For Law and Social Policy.

THE VISITATION CONFLICT

Denial of visitation rights is a big issue for many absent dads and one of the reasons why some don't pay support. **Jeffery Leving,** author of *Fathers' Rights*, puts it this way:

"In situations where mothers are denying visitation or there's no visitation, the vast majority of fathers are delinquent in support. That's a problem. When a father has lost everything — his home, his wife, and then he loses his children — where is the motivation to pay support?"

David L. Levy, president of the Children's Rights Council, said "children are the main victims" when their parents are at war over visitation. He says the child needs the love of both parents. He urges mothers to encourage the children to stay in contact with their dads.

Levy and others believe that visitation rights should be enforced just as child support orders are by the courts and agencies. It's unfair, they say, for a father to have to pay child support when he can't see his kids because of the spitefulness of the mother.

ACES says visitation problems should be resolved outside the courts. "Child support and visitation are separate issues," it says. It favors programs by counselors and social workers to help mediate visitation disputes.

DEADBEATS BEGONE

Casey Hoffman, the child support official-turned-private collector, says "men dodging their child support obligations should be 'called out' by other men as greedy, insensitive, uncaring parents — a sure way to stop the bragging about beating the system."

John Blosser, the National Enquirer reporter who chases down deadbeats, says more media attention is needed to change public attitudes about dads who don't pay. "It's happened on other social problems, like DWI, smoking and even second-hand smoke. The answer is more education, led by the government, to change the way we think, to care about kids and take care of them. I think it's a moral and spiritual problem."

Blosser says he'll know things have changed when "some Bubba is sitting in a bar and tells Billy Bob next to him about how he's not paying his child support. Billy Bob then says to him, 'That tells me you're not much of a man.' "

Expert's Program Would Assure Support For Kids

Irwin Garfinkel is a college professor and author who is a long-time scholar on child poverty and its impact. He advocates a government "child support assurance" program to make sure that children of single moms have a level of financial support to keep them out of poverty.

Garfinkel

Garfinkel believes non-custodial parents should be made to pay. "All parents living apart from their children should be obligated to share income with them," he says.

But when the children suffer because of not enough child support or family income, the government should assure that families receive a minimum payment, Garfinkel says.

Garfinkel is a professor at Columbia University's School of Social Work. He's written about single mothers and their children and the shortcomings of the child support system. He says the inadequate collections breed a greater dependence on welfare.

GARFINKEL'S PROPOSAL HAS THREE MAJOR COMPONENTS:

- *A child support standard using a simple formula for establishing the amount of obligation.*
- *Routine income withholding for child support, administered by the IRS.*
- *An assured benefit payment from the government to children not receiving enough child support from the non-custodial parent.*

"On average, children who grow up in poverty," Garfinkel writes, "are more likely to drop out of school than children who grow up in more affluent circumstances, to conceive children out of wedlock, and to become poor and dependent on welfare as adults."

Before the current child support enforcement system was created in 1974, by amending the Social Security Act, Garfinkel said he thought the effort to collect child support was mainly a way of harassing welfare moms and dads too poor to pay. He thought government "should let well enough alone."

His views changed. He said research convinced him that assurance of child support could relieve economic insecurity and dependence on welfare at little or no extra cost to the government.

Says Garfinkel: "If architects of the Social Security Act could invent a social institution that assured that children were supported by their deceased parent, surely we can invent a social institution to assure that children are supported by their living parents."

Garfinkel is a consultant and researcher for state and federal agencies. Prior to joining Columbia University, he was director of the Institute For Research On Poverty at the University of Wisconsin-Madison.

THE AUTHORS

Rose

Louis J. Rose and Roy Malone are longtime reporters for the St. Louis Post-Dispatch. Over the years they frequently teamed up on investigative stories, often involving public corruption and social issues.

They first bumped into each other while covering a jetliner hijacking at the St. Louis airport. They shared an award from the American Bar Association for stories disclosing how drunk drivers routinely escaped punishment because of a lax judicial system.

Rose is the author of *How To Investigate Your Friends and Enemies,* a book that explores investigative techniques and is full of practical tips for searching paper trails.

An expert in untangling complicated financial dealings, Rose has won many journalism awards, including one from Investigative Reporters and Editors, Inc. He was a Pulitzer Prize finalist for exposing St. Louis' prosecutor who stole city money to pay for prostitutes. Rose retired after 31 years with the Post-Dispatch. He previously worked with the Providence Journal-Bulletin and the Terre Haute (Ind.) Star.

Malone

Roy Malone covered state government as an Associated Press reporter before joining the Post-Dispatch.

He has covered financial and governmental news for the Post-Dispatch and worked on investigative projects ranging from nursing home abuses to political corruption.

During a stint as a television reporter he won an Emmy for a series on the inadequacies of the St. Louis airport.

INDEX

APPENDIX A

STATE CHILD ENFORCEMENT OFFICES

(s) 800 number only statewide
(n) 800 number nationwide

ALABAMA
Department of Human Resources
Division of Child Support
50 Ripley Street
Montgomery, AL 36130-1801
(334) 242-9300
Fax: (334) 242-0606
1 800 284-4347(s)

ALASKA
Child Support Enforcement Division
550 West 7th Avenue, Suite 310
Anchorage, AK 99501-6699
(907) 269-6900
Fax: (907) 269-6813
1 800 478-3300(s)

ARIZONA
Division of Child Support Enforcement
P.O. Box 40458
Phoenix, AZ 85067
(602) 252-4045
(no toll free number)

ARKANSAS
Office of Child Support Enforcement
P.O. Box 8133
Little Rock, AR 72203
(501) 682-8398
Fax: (501) 682-6002
1 800 264-2445(n) payments
1 800 247-4549(n) program

CALIFORNIA
Office of Child Support
Department of Social Services
P. O. Box 944245
Sacramento, CA 95244-2450
(916) 654-1532
Fax: (916) 657-3791
1 800 952-5253(s)

COLORADO
Division of Child Support Enforcement
1575 Sherman Street, 2nd Floor
Denver, CO 80203-1714
(303) 866-5994
Fax: (303) 866-3574
(no toll free number)

CONNECTICUT
Department of Social Services
Bureau of Child Support Enforcement
25 Sigourney Street
Hartford, CT 06106-5033
(860) 424-5251

Fax: (860) 951-2996
1 800 228-5437(n) problems
1 800 647-8872(n) information
1 800 698-0572(n) payments

DELAWARE

Division of Child Support Enforcement
Delaware Health and Social Services
1901 North Dupont Hwy
P.O. Box 904
New Castle, DE 19720
(302) 577-4863, 577-4800
Fax: (302) 577-4873
(no toll free number)

DISTRICT OF COLUMBIA

Office of Paternity and Child Support Enforcement
Department of Human Services
800 9th Street, SW, 2nd Floor
Washington, DC 20024-2485
(202) 645-7500
(no toll free number)

FLORIDA

Child Support Enforcement Program
Department of Revenue
P.O. Box 8030
Tallahassee, FL 32314-8030
(850) 922-9590
Fax: (850) 488-4401
(no toll free number)

GEORGIA

Child Support Administration
P.O. Box 38450
Atlanta, GA 30334-0450
(404) 657-3851
Fax: (404) 657-3326
1 800 227-7993(s)

GUAM

Department of Law
Child Support Enforcement Office
238 Archbishop F.C. Flores, 7th Floor
Agana, GU 96910
(671) 475-3360
(no toll free number)

HAWAII

Child Support Enforcement Agency
Department of Attorney General
680 Iwilei Street, Suite 490
Honolulu, HI 96817
(808) 587-3698
(no toll free number)

IDAHO

Bureau of Child Support Services
Department of Health and Welfare
450 West State Street, 5th

Floor
Boise, ID 83720-5005
(208) 334-5710
Fax: (208) 334-0666
1 800 356-9868(n)

ILLINOIS

Child Support Enforcement Division
Illinois Department of Public Aid
509 South Sixth
Mariott Building
P.O. Box 19405
Springfield, IL 62701-1825
(217) 524-4602
Fax: (217) 524-4608
1 800 447-4278(s)

INDIANA

Child Support Office
402 West Washington Street, Rm W360
Indianapolis, IN 46204
(317) 233-5437
Fax: (317) 233-4925
1 800 622-4932(n)

IOWA

Bureau of Collections
Department of Human Services
Hoover Building, 5th Floor
Des Moines, IA 50319
(515) 281-5580
Fax: (515) 281-8854
(no toll free number)

KANSAS

Child Support Enforcement Program
Department of Social & Rehabilitation Services
P.O. Box 497
Topeka, KS 66601
(913) 296-3237
Fax: (913) 296-5206
1 800 432-0152 withholding
1 800 570-6743 collections
1 800 432-3913 fraud hotline

KENTUCKY

Division of Child Support Enforcement
Cabinet for Families and Children
P.O. Box 2150
Frankfort, KY 40602
(502) 564-2285
Fax: (502) 564-5988

LOUISIANA

Support Enforcement Services
Office of Family Support
P. O. Box 94065
Baton Rouge, LA 70804-4065
(504) 342-4780
Fax: (504) 342-7397
1 800 256-4650(s) payments

MAINE

Division of Support Enforce-

ment and Recovery
Bureau of Family Independence
Department of Human Services
State House Station 11 Whitten Road
Augusta, ME 04333
(207) 287-2886
Fax: (207) 287-5096
1 800 371-3101(s)

MARYLAND

Child Support Enforcement Administration
Department of Human Resources
311 West Saratoga Street
Baltimore, MD 21201
(410) 767-7619
Fax: (410) 333-8992
1 800 332-6347(s)

MASSACHUSETTS

Child Support Enforcement Division
Department of Revenue
141 Portland Street
Cambridge, MA 02139-1937
Fax: (617) 621-4991
1 800 332-2733(n)

MICHIGAN

Office of Child Support
Department of Social Services
P.O. Box 30478
Lansing, MI 48909-7978
(517) 373-7570
Fax: (517) 373-4980
(no toll free number)

MINNESOTA

Office of Child Support Enforcement
Department of Human Services
444 Lafayette Road, 4th Floor
St. Paul, MN 55155-3846
(612) 215-1714
Fax: (612) 297-4450
(no toll free number)

MISSISSIPPI

Division of Child Support Enforcement
Department of Human Services
P.O. Box 352
Jackson, MS 39205
(601) 359-4861
Fax: (601) 359-4415
1 800 434-5437(n) (Jackson)
1 800 354-6039 (Hines, Rankin and Madison counties)

MISSOURI

Department of Social Services
Division of Child Support Enforcement
P.O. Box 2320
Jefferson City, MO 65102-2320

(573) 751-4301
Fax: (573) 751-8450
1 800 859-7999(n)

MONTANA

Child Support Enforcement Division
Department of Public Health and Human Services
P.O. Box 202943
Helena, MT 59620
(406) 442-7278
1 800 346-5437(s)

NEBRASKA

Child Support Enforcement Office
Department of Social Services
P.O. Box 95044
Lincoln, NE 68509
(402) 471-9160
Fax: (402) 471-9455
1 800 831-4573(s)

NEVADA

Child Support Enforcement Program
Nevada State Welfare Division
2527 North Carson Street
Carson City, NV 89706-0113
(702) 687-4744
Fax: (702) 684-8026
1 800 992-0900(s)

NEW HAMPSHIRE

Office of Child Support
Division of Human Services
Health and Human Services Building
6 Hazen Drive
Concord, NH 03301-6531
(603) 271-4427
Fax: (603) 271-4787
1 800 852-3345, ext. 4427(s)

NEW JERSEY

Division of Family Development
Department of Human Services
Bureau of Child Support and Paternity Programs
P.O. Box 716
Trenton, NJ 08625-0716
(609) 588-2915
Fax: (609) 588-3369
1 800 621-5437(n)

NEW MEXICO

Child Support Enforcement Bureau
Department of Human Services
P.O. Box 25109
Santa Fe, NM 87504
(505) 827-7200
Fax: (505) 827-7285
1 800 432-6217(s)

NEW YORK

Office of Child Support Enforcement

Department of Social Services
P.O. Box 14
One Commerce Plaza
Albany, NY 12260-0014
(518) 474-9081
Fax: (518) 486-3127
1 800 343-8859(s)

NORTH CAROLINA

Child Support Enforcement Office
Division of Social Services
Department of Human Resources
100 East Six Forks Road
Raleigh, NC 27609-7750
(919) 571-4114
Fax: (919) 881-2280
1 800 992-9457(s)

NORTH DAKOTA

Department of Human Services
Child Support Enforcement Agency
P.O. Box 7190
Bismarck, ND 58507-7190
(701) 328-3582
Fax: (701) 328-5497
1 800 755-8530(s)

OHIO

Office of Family Assistance and Child Support Enforcement
Department of Human Services
30 East Broad Street, 31st Floor
Columbus, OH 43266-0423
(614) 752-6561
Fax: (614) 752-9760
1 800 686-1556

OKLAHOMA

Child Support Enforcement Division
Department of Human Services
P.O. Box 53552
Oklahoma City, OK 73152
(405) 522-5871
Fax: (405) 522-2753
1 800 522-2922(n)

OREGON

Recovery Services Section
Adult and Family Services Division
Department of Human Resources
260 Liberty Street N.E.
Salem, OR 97310
(503) 378-5567
Fax: (503) 391-5526
1 800 850-0228(s)
1 800 850-0294 (s) rotary

PENNSYLVANIA

Bureau of Child Support Enforcement
Department of Public Welfare
P.O. Box 8018

Harrisburg, PA 17105
(717) 787-3672
Fax: (717) 787-9706
1 800 932-0211(n)

PUERTO RICO
Child Support Enforcement
Department of Social Services
P.O. Box 9023349
San Juan, PR 00902-3349
(787) 767-1500
Fax: (787) 282-7411
(no toll free number)

RHODE ISLAND
Child Support Services
Division of Administration and Taxation
77 Dorrance Street
Providence, RI 02903
(401) 277-2847
Fax: (401) 277-6674
1 800 638-5437(s)

SOUTH CAROLINA
Department of Social Services
Child Support Enforcement Division
P.O. Box 1469
Columbia, SC 29202-1469
(803) 737-5875
Fax: (803) 737-6032
1 800 768-5858(n)
1 800 768-6779(s) payments

SOUTH DAKOTA
Office of Child Support Enforcement
Department of Social Services
700 Governor's Drive
Pierre, SD 57501-2291
(605) 773-3641
Fax: (605) 773-5246
(no toll free number)

TENNESSEE
Child Support Services
Department of Human Services
Citizens Plaza Building, 12th Floor
400 Deadrick Street
Nashville, TN 37248-7400
(615) 313-4880
Fax: (615) 532-2791
1 800 838-6911(s) payments

TEXAS
Office of the Attorney General
State Office
Child Support Division
P.O. Box 12017
Austin, TX 78711-2017
(512) 460-6000
Fax: (512) 479-6478
1 800 252-8014(n)

UTAH
Office of Recovery Services
P.O. Box 45011
Salt Lake City, UT 84145-

0011
(801) 536-8500
Fax: (801) 436-8509
1 800 257-9156(n)

VERMONT

Office of Child Support
103 South Main Street
Waterbury, VT 05671-1901
Fax: (802) 244-1483
1 800 786-3214(n)

VIRGIN ISLANDS

Paternity and Child Support Division
Department of Justice
GERS Building, 2nd Floor
48B-50C Krondprans Gade
St. Thomas, VI 00802
(809) 775-3070
Fax: (809) 775-3808
(no toll free number)

VIRGINIA

Division of Child Support Enforcement
Department of Social Services
730 East Broad Street
Richmond, VA 23219
(804) 692-1428
Fax: (804) 692-1405
1 800 468-8894(s)

WASHINGTON

Division of Child Support
Department of Social Health Services
P.O. Box 9162
Olympia, WA 98504-9162
(360) 664-5000
Fax: (360) 664-5209-10
1 800 457-6202(n)

WEST VIRGINIA

Child Support Enforcement Division
Department of Health & Human Resources
1900 Kanawha Boulevard East
Capitol Complex, Building 6, Room 817
Charleston, WV 25305
(304) 558-3780
1 800 249-3778(n)

WISCONSIN

Bureau of Child Support
Division of Economic Support
P.O. Box 7935
Madison, WI 53707-7935
(608) 266-9909
Fax: (608) 267-2824
(no toll free number)

WYOMING

Child Support Enforcement
Department of Family Services
2300 Capital Avenue, 3rd Fl.
Cheyenne, WY 82002-0490
(307) 777-6948
Fax: (307) 777-3693
(no toll free number)

APPENDIX B

REGIONAL CHILD SUPPORT ENFORCEMENT OFFICES

Region I — Connecticut, Maine, Massachusetts, New Hampshire, Rhode Island, Vermont

OCSE Program Manager
Administration for Children and Families
John F. Kennedy Federal Building
Room 2000
Boston, MA 02203
(617) 565-2478

Region II — New York, New Jersey, Puerto Rico, Virgin Islands

OCSE Program Manager
Administration for Children and Families
Federal Building, Room 4048
26 Federal Plaza
New York, NY 10278
(212) 264-2890

Region III — Delaware, Maryland, Pennsylvania, Virginia, West Virginia, District of Columbia

OCSE Program Manager
Administration for Children and Families
P.O. Box 8436
Philadelphia, PA 19104
(215) 596-4370

Region IV — Alabama, Florida, Georgia, Kentucky, Mississippi, North Carolina, South Carolina, Tennessee

OCSE Program Manager
Administration for Children and Families
101 Marietta Tower, Suite 821
Atlanta, GA 30323
(404) 331-2180

Region V — Illinois, Indiana, Michigan, Minnesota, Ohio, Wisconsin

OCSE Program Manager
Administration for Children and Families
105 W. Adams Street, 20th Floor
Chicago, IL 60603
(312) 353-4237

Region VI — Arkansas, Louisiana, New Mexico, Oklahoma, Texas

OCSE Program Manager
Administration for Children and Families
1301 Young Street, Room 945

(ACF-3)
Dallas, TX 75202
(214) 767-3749

Region VII — Iowa, Kansas, Missouri, Nebraska

OCSE Program Manager
Administration for Children and Families
601 East 12th Street
Federal Building, Suite 276
Kansas City, MO 64106
(816) 426-3584

Region VIII — Colorado, Montana, North Dakota, South Dakota, Utah, Wyoming

OCSE Program Manager
Administration for Children and Families
Federal Office Building
1961 Stout Street, Room 325
Denver, CO 80294-3538
(303) 844-3100

Region IX — Arizona, California, Hawaii, Nevada, Guam

OCSE Program Manager
Administration for Children and Families
50 United Nations Plaza
Room 450
San Francisco, CA 94102
(415) 437-8459

Region X — Alaska, Idaho, Oregon, Washington

OCSE Program Manager
Administration for Children and Families
2201 Sixth Avenue
Mail Stop RX-70
Seattle, WA 98121
(206) 615-2547